Let Me Tell You a Story

Elfie F. Salisbury

ISBN 978-1-68517-509-2 (paperback)
ISBN 978-1-68517-510-8 (digital)

Christian Faith Publishing, Inc.
832 Park Avenue
Meadville, PA 16335
www.christianfaithpublishing.com

Printed in the United States of America

Foreword

Ms. Salisbury is the youngest of seventeen children. In this book, she has shared her deepest sorrows and biggest achievements. The wisdom she has is beyond her years. *Let Me Tell You a Story* is a book that will guide you through each day. Her words will make you feel like she's a part of your family. As I am proud to say, she's a part of mine.

Thank you, Aunt Elfie, for all the years of hearing what I had to say, understanding my ideas, and validating my dreams. I love you.

—Christina L. Parks

Food for the soul requires more than an occasional snack or your favorite menu. Consume what is good for you even if it's difficult to swallow.

Growing up in a small town, we always had lots of choices of churches to attend. Many different denominations dotted our city and kept us culturally sound. Not knowing what those denominations entailed or practiced was sort of scary to me as a kid. I was taught one way and one way only. I was led to believe that those who didn't practice my "religion" didn't truly believe in God or the Bible.

As I grew older, and I mean much older, I came to realize how false my beliefs actually were. I realized so much about people, myself, God, and religion when I realized Who God really was. God was not the punisher. He was not ready to strike me dead at any moment that I messed up. He truly loved me. God was so full of love for everyone, not just those who attended my church. He cared for me every step of the way.

I was taught from the King James Version of the Bible. I was always told that it was the only true Word of God. It was difficult to understand, but thankfully, I learned to understand it. Starting at a young age, I began reading the Bible. In the huge family Bible that lay open on our coffee table, I found a reading schedule that walked me through the entire Bible in a year. So I read every day. I began reading through the Bible at about ten years old. I was committed, and, yes, I did it.

Since that time, I have committed to reading through the Bible almost every year. By now, I have read the Old and New Testaments about forty times. My commitment had not always been about the content but more about the accomplishment. Gradually, I have learned to appreciate the stories and wisdom that unfold through every single page. I pray for God to help me understand. He does.

Even though I've read through so many times, I still gain insights and have those aha moments.

In order to grow in the Word of God, read the Bible. There are so many different versions that help you study and understand the passages. Use a study Bible that helps interpret the words. Dig a little deeper by using apps or media that help you reflect and interpret what you're reading. It's not hard, but it does take some effort to stay with it. Challenge yourself to learn something every single day. Reflect on what you read. How can you apply it to your life to become a better person?

Don't always believe what you are told about the scripture. Study God's word for yourself so you will know what is good and right and true. We all have those verses that we can recite verbatim. If you want to grow as a Christian, enhance your knowledge. Stop snacking on tidbits of sermons and feasting off the same menu of stories you learned as a child. Get to the real meat that feeds your soul. It may not always be what you like to hear, but the Word will sharpen your Christian walk.

Swallow the hard stuff that challenges you to be a better person and may change your childhood beliefs. Enhance your Christian walk by reading the Word. Let it shape you into being the best godly person you can be.

Challenge: Read through the Bible in a year. Learn as much as you can. Apply it to your life. Enjoy God's Word.

Love is amazing. True love is endless. Unconditional love is God.

Understanding love is a chore in itself. Trying to figure out what love actually is can be a challenging task. I am the youngest of seventeen children. If you asked me if I was loved, yes, I was. The way I was shown love was food on the table, clothes on my body, a roof over my head, and occasional hugs. Growing up, my family rarely said "I love you" to each other. I know my mom and dad loved each other, but I never saw it. They were not affectionate at all in front of us or anyone else. So we grew up unaffectionate. Personal talks about love, puberty, and sex were never a topic in our house. They were a taboo.

My dad never told me he loved me. He would say "be careful" but never "I love you." I guess that was his way of letting me know his feelings. My mom softened up a bit in her old age. When I was child, she was always trying to put me on her lap and hold me. Eventually, I got too big. She never really told me she loved me until I was an adult. When I heard other people say it to each other, I always thought it was a personal thing that should never be spoken in public where anyone could hear it. It was sort of shocking.

Love comes in many forms. I saw it with my own eyes. I heard it with my ears. I perked up because I had never really seen it in action. As a kid, I was amazed that people loved each other. When someone told me they loved me, I doubted them. I was always trying to find the reason they did. I was baffled. No one really took the time to explain it. I learned to love others. I had the feeling in my chest of respect and compassion for others. That was love. When I served others, that was love. I was getting used to accepting it and also giving it. I felt more comfortable.

I had read about true love. I had seen it in movies. I thought I found it once but was mistaken. I remember liking certain guys in school. They were crushes and infatuations, not true love. I didn't really date until college, but I knew there was a different kind of love happening. It wasn't like loving my family and friends; I found a companion. I thought I could love him forever. I dreamed of having a life together with him. Then it went away. My opportunity for true love escaped me. It wasn't meant to be.

I found unconditional love in God. I had heard stories in the Bible growing up in Sunday school about the compassion God had for people. I heard how He rescued people and fought for them, but I really didn't understand it as love. As an adult, I realized what it was. Humans don't have unconditional love like God. Unconditional means that no matter what, God will never turn His back on you. God will never give up on you. God will always be there for you. It's difficult to grasp that concept because if a human can achieve unconditional love status, it's rare.

Only when I thought about the stories in the Bible where God rescued people or parted the seas for them, or even sent His own Son, Jesus, to die on a Cross for our sins, did I realize how much He truly loves us unconditionally. The greatest gift was Jesus, Who came as a baby and grew to be a Savior of the world. The greatest form of love was letting Jesus bear the sins of the entire world and die a human death to save us. Having Jesus leave heaven to save those who didn't even love God had to be love. Think about it.

God loved us so much that He gave His only Son to die for us and still has our backs when we mess up. That is unconditional love. He runs after us and seeks us out because He loves us. Don't forget it.

Challenge: Don't be afraid to tell someone you love them. Love those you don't even know. Love your enemies, and pray for them. You could be the only connection to God that they know.

Be who you were meant to be. Don't be distracted by what other people think of you. Live life.

Many times, I've thought about what it was like being a stupid kid. Just in the sense that I lived life but was navigating through waters that were so uncertain. I thought I knew it all. I thought I was doing what was best for me. I was a kid. I hadn't even started a resume of life's journey. I was at the beginning.

As an adult, I look back thinking how foolish I was to think the way I did or even act the way I did. If I could go back and tell myself a few things, I would. I was so caught up in what others thought of me. I was very peer conscious. I worried about my reputation even in middle school. My teen years should have had more meaning. I should have had more fun instead of calculating every single move.

In middle school, I was an athlete. I wasn't really allowed to play on a sports team, because my mom didn't want to cart me to and from practice. In eighth grade, the school formed the first ever girls' basketball team. I was asked to participate by one of the coaches. I wanted to. I had never played regulation ball on any team. I grew up around my brother and his friends, so I knew how to play the game. I was scared. My mom said yes.

We had an amazing team and went undefeated through the season. I played like I knew how. I scored eighteen points the very first game. I was a natural. I didn't really care about much, because I was a good athlete and showed what I could do. I was a good student too. I never let my ego get the best of me. I was a humble kid. I loved pleasing others, and I hated losing. We lost in the tournament round and took third place that first year after a tremendous first season.

The transition to high school meant that I would have to compete with older kids for a position on the team. I would have a brand-new coach whom I didn't know. She was awesome but yelled a lot. I heard about her reputation. She scared me. I shut down. I was a skilled player, but I sat on the bench because I was intimidated and afraid that I would mess up. I lived with that fear for years. I couldn't get it together because of what others thought of me. I allowed others to intimidate me out of having fun.

Sometimes I think back to those years of confusion and navigation. I wondered what my life would have been like if I had cared less about what people thought about me and more about having fun. I wondered what it would have been like to be able to do the *don't* that I had been told all my life would take me to hell. I had no desire to drink, smoke, or do drugs; but just being able to center my life with some activities that didn't revolve around church would have been nice. During my teen years, I moved closer to committing myself to religion and having less of a desire for school activities. The balance shifted.

God makes each of us uniquely. We are who we are because of Him. I believe that God had a purpose for my life. I didn't understand it at the time, and I was too busy worrying about people and lost sight of my purpose. All of the what-ifs still float through my mind. It doesn't matter how I got to where I am today; I made it. I stopped worrying about what people think of me many years ago. Sometimes, it hurts when the brutal past comes up. Memories are reminders that God is focused on me no matter what I think, feel, or care. God's sole purpose for me is a new page written every day of my life. I wish I knew that as a kid.

Be who you are meant to be. Live life as if each day is your last. Love greatly. Accept your purpose.

Challenge: Don't be distracted by the negativity. Live life to the fullest each day. Find your purpose, and share it with others. Live. Laugh. Dance.

God created good in all of us—even in an evil, jealous, vindictive person you will find good. You just have to look for it a little harder.

As children, we are very trusting of individuals. In a large family like mine, I was very trusting of everyone. Neighbors, friends, family, church family, teachers, they were all trusted individuals. I am the youngest of seventeen kids, so I was around but sort of got lost in the shuffle. Everyone knew I was there, but they also thought someone else was looking out for me.

I grew up in an age where you could knock on a neighbor's door and enter the house without fear of being there. I could ride my bike around the block without fear of someone taking me. I could hang out with the neighbor kids and play on the street until dark without the fear of being hurt. Neighborhoods were friendly, and everyone knew everyone's business. We had trusted family friends.

I remember taking a road trip with my cousins to Kentucky one cold winter. I barely knew them but trusted that they would make sure I was safe. I was. I was cold but safe. I would spend the night at my best friend's house without any thought of being hurt. I was cared for. I remember going to slumber parties and hanging with kids from school. We had fun, and we were safe.

I was asked to go on an overnight camping trip with a friend of the family whose son went to school with me. It was just down the road. The guy worked with my dad, so he had been to our house several times and probably went to church with us too. He had a camper at a small fishing hole on the south end of town. His two sons were going too. We were just going to fish, hang out by the little pond, and have fun. That night changed my life forever.

I woke up in the middle of the night and realized something wasn't right. The guy had taken advantage of me at eight years old. I didn't understand what was going on and desperately tried to go back to sleep to pretend it wasn't happening. Everyone else was asleep. Someone I trusted had hurt me mentally, physically, and emotionally. I was eight years old and in shock.

I knew that if I told anyone, it would be my fault and I would be in trouble. I never told. I shut down because I was confused about the situation. My demeanor changed. I didn't feel comfortable around others, and I didn't want to be touched. I really had a hard time letting anyone take my picture too. I thought it was my fault and that I had done something wrong. I lived with guilt until I finally told someone in my early twenties. By then, it was too late to do anything to the guy. He had moved away not long after that.

I grew up an emotional wreck. I had all of the signs and symptoms of an abused child. I never told. I went through middle school, high school, and most of my college years harboring guilt. I was certain it was my fault. After I told a close friend, the situation played out like it wasn't important and I had to get over it. I didn't. Many years later, I finally got counseling and learned that the guy had died many years earlier. I was relieved. I often wondered what I would say to him after all those years if I had run into him as an adult.

Was there good in this person? He was one of the most kind, gentle, and caring individuals you could ever meet. He was very soft-spoken and a good dad to his boys. I forgave him. I had to move on with my life. It was difficult finding any good in this individual who had wrecked my life at eight years old. When I became an adult, it became much easier to forgive. Do the same. Scars are the result of our battles and reminders of our fights.

Challenge: Find the good in every single individual. Look for it. Forgive them. You will suffer more than they will if you don't.

When God holds you in His hand, it's difficult to roll off the edge and out of His reach.

I've seen artist's renditions of God's hands. They look mighty and strong. As a kid, I couldn't imagine God's hands being big enough to hold the whole world! That song used to baffle my little mind. How could God's hands be the size to shape a small figure into a human from dust? How could I ever reach out to God's hand with my tiny fingers and expect Him to grasp them? But He does.

When I feel like I am at a loss for words because I am so troubled about life or I'm going through a bad spot where my faith is being tested, I imagine God holding me. I imagine being curled up in a fetal position being gently rocked back and forth by God. It's then that I understand that I have His full protection and I can rest without worries. It's then that I understand that nothing can come against me. He shields me.

Most of my young life was spent in the hand of God. I was sexually assaulted around age eight. My young mind couldn't grasp the feeling of guilt that I had somehow caused this thing to happen. I was too scared to say anything to my parents, because I thought it was somehow my fault and I would get punished. I kept it to myself. Gently, I swayed back and forth in God's hand. He soothed me.

During my adolescent years, when I should have been having fun and trying my wings, I kept to myself. No one knew but God. I had to live with the emotional stress and turmoil every single day. I wondered if other kids even knew what I felt like or went through the same thing I did. It was a constant daily battle. I wondered if it showed in my face or if I said something to tip anyone off. It was an emotion that I tucked safely deep down inside myself and didn't tell anyone. Gently, God rocked me back and forth.

As a teenager, I didn't want to be touched, nor did I show any physical affection toward others. I fought with my emotions every single day. Something would trigger that awful, gut-wrenching memory, and I would relive it all over again. While others were having a good time, I kept my emotions in check and turned inward even more. No one knew. I had people I could have trusted enough to say something to, but then I thought about having to face the individual. Nope, I wasn't ready. I lay curled up in God's big hands.

As an adult, I began dating. I was very leery about everyone and everything. My emotions kept me in check to the point that I was more relieved about cutting off relationships than having to tell someone or explain why I was acting weird. It was very uncomfortable. I never really outgrew it. I was reliving an event that consumed my life. It changed my whole perspective on things. I was constantly asking God to forgive me. It wasn't my fault. God held me in His hands.

The release came after I received professional therapy. I was also told that the individual had passed away. It's like my life took a breath of fresh air. I felt the weighted burden lifted off my shoulders. My fear was that I would have to come face-to-face with someone who hurt me and how I would respond. I was free. God let me gently climb out of His hand and walk again. God has carried me my whole life. The daily struggles were just too much to bear. God was the only one I could depend on and trust.

Nowadays, when I go through a struggle, I climb back into His hand. I have a familiar spot between the creases and folds. He gently rocks me back to reality and helps me get my footing. God will never allow me to fall off the edge. He's my protector. I learned that He's always within my reach.

Challenge: There's nothing too big for God. When you feel the need, climb into His hands and rest.

God blesses us with different gifts. Accept yours, and use it to help others and glorify Him.

Have you ever sat back and really thought about all of the gifts and talents that God has given you? Think of the special things that you can do that others admire. Think about the particular skill set that you have that others around you don't have. Think about the things you are "good" at and you perform easily while others struggle in the same situations. Those things are your gifts and talents.

Every good and perfect gift comes from God. Even the most wretched individuals have talents and gifts. Think about those who are evil. They also have talents and gifts. Now does everyone use their talents and gifts to glorify God? Probably not. We witness very talented and gifted individuals who cause harm and even rob others of their abilities to shine. Is there a limit on how many gifts and talents we can have? I don't think so. The Bible tells us to ask and we will receive. The thing is, how many people take time to ask?

I have always thought that God blessed me with wisdom at a very early age. I remember sitting in Sunday school classes and absorbing the stories from the Bible. They were taught from the King James Version of the Bible. So my teachers taught using the visual flannelgraph boards. I could visualize the stories coming to life. I loved learning about the Bible. After I learned to read, I was so eager to read the Bible for myself. I had a little New Testament, so if I wanted to read the Old Testament, I pulled out the family Bible.

As a kid, reading the King James Version of the Bible was tough. The translation was difficult to understand because it was written in the old language that used unfamiliar words. We weren't allowed to have any other version of the Bible in the house. It was King James or nothing. So I prayed for understanding, and God honored my prayer. I could actually understand the verses and stories that I read. I would ask questions in Sunday school that my teachers tried to answer, but I could tell they were struggling. I didn't mean to put them on the spot; I really had a thirst for knowledge.

As I grew older, my thirst for learning the scriptures never changed. I had read through the entire Bible at about age thirteen.

I found a reading schedule in the big family Bible for the year. So I did it. I remember stumbling over scriptures and stories in the Bible, praying for God to help me understand, and then it happened. He actually helped me understand what I was reading. It's almost like I had the most perfect insight into the words that others didn't have. That's where my questions in Sunday school came from.

God didn't just stop there. Over the years, I began to ask for God to bless me with talents and gifts. I picked up playing the piano without lessons. Through that, God blessed me to write songs. God blessed me with a voice to sing my songs. He blessed me to be able to teach others and be a leader. I was blessed with the ability to write stories and communicate very well on paper. That helped during college. God blessed me with more than I even asked for. I can't begin to name them all.

I can say that I have never misused my gifts and talents. I'm sure sometimes people look at me and don't understand my way of thinking, but it's also a gift. I have used my gifts and abilities to glorify God. I also believe that since I was faithful with what He had blessed me with, He knew I could handle more. So I was given even more. Some took a little encouragement to hone, but they, too, flourished.

If you lack wisdom and understanding, God will give it to you. Just ask. One day, you will wake up and find out that you have a new interest or the ability to do something new. Just accept it and use it for good.

Challenge: Ask God to help you, and He will. Ask for understanding, He will bless you. The most difficult part is asking. He's waiting on you.

Parents aren't always perfect, but they still deserve honor.

If you're a parent, you understand the demands of being a role model, provider, nurse, doctor, chauffeur, encourager, cheerleader, disciplinarian, and much more. You love your kids no matter what. It's the way God is to us. He has unconditional love for us regardless of when we screw up. It's difficult, as a parent, to watch your kids go through the struggles of growing up. The process can be so overwhelming.

My parents weren't perfect. In fact, they both finished school with an eighth-grade education. They were both working and caring for others when they were just teenagers. My dad was the oldest of seven children, and my mom was an only child. Since my mom was caring for others' children, she decided she could just start a family of her own and care for them. So they married young, and my mom had her first child when she was sixteen years old. Sixteen other children came along over the next thirty years.

When I listen to the stories about the older brothers and sisters and how they were raised in the hills of Kentucky, I am so very glad that I was number seventeen. I was fortunate to grow up with indoor plumbing, electricity, and other common amenities that the others may not have been privy to. We didn't starve to death, and we had a roof over our heads and clothes on our backs. My parents were hard workers who taught us the value of money and work.

My mother was forty-five years old when I was born. My dad was five years older. By the time I was a teenager, they were focused on retirement. That was very difficult for me. I had learned to become self-sufficient by the time I was in middle school and took care of myself. I believe my mother suffered from anxiety and depression, so she slept a lot, as far as I can remember. My dad worked as a carpenter all day and then came home to tend the most beautiful vegetable gardens you had ever seen. That was my life.

I was left alone to make sure my clothes were washed, schoolwork was completed, and I made it on the bus for school every single day. When I was a teenager, not being able to go anywhere except church and church activities was a little stifling. We made it to church every time the doors were open. That was a priority in our family and at our house. I never really appreciated my parents' roles and efforts until I was an adult.

I knew better than to disrespect my parents. I had learned the commandment to honor my father and mother, so I did. Did I always agree with them? Heck, no, I didn't. I went through a stage during my teenage years that I severely disliked my parents. I hated the situation when they moved away from my hometown. I had one more high school year to go, and I couldn't understand the benefit of tearing up my life. I moved, but I made their lives miserable because I was miserable.

As an adult, I learned to appreciate the values and principles that my parents had instilled in me. I learned what a solid work ethic could get me and that honesty really was the best policy. I learned that keeping God at the center of my life and surrounding myself with family and support were essential for living. I learned the value of money and being able to afford and buy the things I needed.

Did I always honor my parents? Sadly, no. In fits of anger, mistrust, and disbelief, I chose to take the low road. If I could change things, I would, but I believe that growing up allows us to honor our parents when we become parents and truly understand the sacrifices they made for our well-being. I learned to love them and honor them. I just wish they were still around so that we could talk one more time. I think they would be proud of what I've become.

Challenge: Honor your father and your mother that your days on earth will be extended. Love them.

I will praise God, for I am fearfully and wonderfully made (Ps. 139:4).

I've often wondered why I was born into the family I was. I wondered why I live in the country that I do without fear of my life every day like others. There is a distinct purpose for my life. I realize that there is no one else like me. I am unique. I have been gifted with qualities and talents unlike someone else. I am a mixture of genetic materials that exist uniquely to me. I am where I am for a reason and purpose. I am wonderfully and beautifully made.

Going through the lessons in my life helped me to understand that if it was someone else in my shoes going through the same experience, they may not have had the fortitude and boldness to survive and overcome. God knew what He was doing. He has all along. I believe He sent me to earth on a mission for my family and friends. My life has been one lifelong experience and educational experience just to help others survive and make it. I have been and will be an example of God's goodness, grace, and mercy until I die.

Have I always taken my life lessons well? No. Have I questioned God? Yes, I have. Did I wonder why He allowed me to go through things that I felt were unfair? Yes, I did. In hindsight, those were the most important lessons so that I could put myself into someone else's situation. Each lesson was and has been an experience to help at least one person.

When I hear stories of what people are going through, I quickly nod in agreement in my head because I've honestly been there. When I listen and then respond that I truly understand, it's reassuring to them. There's an immediate spiritual bond because it was God's intention all along. My reassurance gives them hope. My experience helps me give them ways to overcome or cope. That's part of my mission.

When I say "wonderfully and beautifully made," I don't mean my physical appearance. I have always hated the shape of my nose. I got it from my mom. When I was younger, I was very self-conscious of it. As I grew older, I learned to accept it. To me, it's still not beautiful, but, hey, it's what I was given. I can live with it. There are other physical attributes I'm not too fond of either, but I've learned to accept who I am.

When I am wonderfully and beautifully made, I believe, for me, it's my spiritual makeup. God has given me a very tender heart for Him and a servant's heart for others. God has given me the ability to make people feel comfortable talking about difficult situations that they never would have opened up about. God has given me the ability to draw close to troubled kids and those who struggle in school. I accept my gifts.

God looks on the inside of me, not necessarily the outside. Being a tomboy, I never wore makeup or dressed in fancy girly clothes. I enjoyed my T-shirts, jeans, and sneakers. I still do. I may not look like much on the outside, but my warm smile draws people in. My tender heart loves the unlovely and gives to those overlooked. God knew exactly what He was doing when He formed me. He knew what I would do and be even before I was born. He had a unique plan all along.

David wrote these words in Psalms. David had God's heart. They had a special relationship. I like to think of myself the same. My relationship with God is unique. Just like David, I am beautiful in God's eyes. I may not be everything to everybody, but I am something to somebody. If I get through to just one person, I've accomplished my mission. Follow God's lead. You're wonderfully and beautifully made for a reason.

Challenge: Be who God wants you to be, not what someone else wants you to be. You have the fingerprint of God on your life. You have a unique beauty like no other.

Learn to pray. It doesn't have to be eloquent; just speak from your heart.

Praying is direct communication with God. Anyone can pray anywhere and at any time. The good thing about God is that He doesn't sleep. He's omniscient and omnipresent. That simply means He can be everywhere at the same time. How that happens, I'm not sure, but I know it. Praying is communication with God. It adds credence to a strong spiritual relationship with Him.

Growing up, we always prayed over our food and thanked God for blessing us. Sometimes, the prayers were simple and quick because we were very hungry. At times, we truly reverenced God for His blessings and the food we had before us. Either way, we gave thanks. I learned to pray my first prayers at the dinner table with words I learned in Sunday school. That was just what I needed as a kid.

Every night, before I went to sleep, I knelt beside my bed and talked with God. Since I was alone with Him, my prayers changed. I wasn't rushing. I simply thanked Him for the blessings and also asked for Him to take care of my family, pets, and the long list of relatives. I prayed the standard prayer of "Now I lay me down to sleep" and then added my own version of thanks. When I was a kid, it worked for me.

As I developed a relationship with God, I learned that I didn't always have to be kneeling to talk with Him. I still prayed in reverence on my knees beside my bed, but I also found myself praying at school, driving, when I was out walking, standing at the foul line shooting a free throw, and even during exams. Any time was a good time. If I needed help, God was like a hero who swept in to save me. He was the only thing I could trust to be there all the time and in any situation.

I learned that I didn't need fancy words to pray. God knew my heart. I wasn't trying to think of words to impress Him; I just simply talked with Him. Sometimes, the fewer words were better. I listened. My simple words and prayers as a child grew up. I had different situations to deal with in my life, so that required different words and emotions. Sometimes, I just wept before God. No words needed.

Learning to pray is easy. God is not so far away that He can't hear you. You can talk with Him just like you talk with anyone else. It's not a one-way conversation. He will answer you. You have to listen, though. He knows your needs and thoughts even before you go to Him. God loves hearing your voice. He loves your transparency. He's not impressed by how well you can speak. Talking with God should be as easy as having a conversation with a friend. You don't check your words when you speak with a friend, so don't do it with God.

Don't ever be embarrassed to pray. The best place to pray is around and with others. Sometimes, the words of your prayer are an encouragement. When people are hurting, they don't care how you pray; they just need your prayers. Praying with individuals allows them to see your transparency with God. They recognize that your prayer edifies a close relationship with Him. Openly praying helps others to build confidence in their own prayer life.

I still kneel beside my bed before I go to sleep at night. I still kneel beside my bed every morning. When I pray on my knees, I'm not distracted. I can focus on God. Throughout the day, I am walking and talking with God. I'm not ashamed if I'm heard. I have prayed openly with colleagues on my school campus. I'm not the best prayer warrior, but I do know how to get to the point with God. Mostly, I'm talking with Him because I love Him. I am thankful for my blessings. Praying is simply talking with God. The more you pray, the easier the words pour out of you. Relax. God simply loves hearing your voice.

Challenge: Find a place to focus on God and pray. Establish your prayer life. Get into a routine.

Quit playing hide-and-seek with God. You hide when He needs you but seek Him when you need something.

When I was a kid, we had so much fun playing hide-and-seek. Since there were so many of us, along with the neighbor kids, we would wait until dusk and let the games begin. The whole neighborhood was our playground. Playing the game at dusk was even better because of low lights. We had a blast. Finally, the "all in free" could be heard in the air, and those who weren't found left their hiding places.

Have you ever wanted to just hide to be alone and regroup? Most of us who are introverts rely on solitude to recharge our batteries. That can require much sleep and rest. Since my job requires me to talk and explain things all day—I'm a teacher—I enjoy getting into my car with quiet silence. I turn on the radio and listen. No talking, just listening. When I get home, I rest and relax. No talking. I listen.

There are times when I purposely hide to regroup, and then there are times I hide from certain individuals. You know those people. I find solace in my classroom. Wandering around just puts me into a position of interaction with others. Sometimes, I just don't feel it. When I'm ready, I am very good at entertaining others. Unfortunately, I wear my emotions outside. Sometimes, people know to just let me go.

With God, there's rarely a time when I've hidden away from Him. I can remember being young and programmed into believing that I had to share Jesus with anyone and everyone. Sometimes, I didn't feel it. Sometimes, God's direction pointed me to someone who really needed Him, and I listened. I had to learn to listen to God and take directions. Not every opportunity was a pleasant encounter. God prepares the hearts of those who are ready to listen and inviting. I've had doors shut in my face because I mentioned Jesus.

We all do good deeds throughout our day. I have helped strangers in parking lots, on the median in the street, in the store, and any other time God compels me. I know it's God. I listen. I feel that familiar tug in my heart to do something. I don't really think I know a stranger. I've learned to be myself, and if an opportunity arises, I share God. God opens the doors. I walk through. I am listening.

When I think about all the times that I've done what God needed me to do, I don't feel so bad asking for His help. It's not that I do good deeds just to feel good about asking for something; it's the fact that God knows me. If I'm willing to listen to Him and follow His lead, my faith is built up. If I was that person who needed help, I know God would send someone my way. I know I would see a miracle. It's reciprocating. God blesses us for blessing others.

There are people who aren't open to doing God's will yet expect Him to get them out of a jam. I don't know how He deals with it. God doesn't ask much of us. He actually blesses us with more than we deserve. It's not like He's asking us to perform major feats, just share if an opportunity arises. If we're always asking for help, maybe it's expected that at some point we need to learn to stand on our own. We're growing physically, so why not spiritually? We have to be secure enough to take advantage of "God opportunities."

Can God rely on you to help someone in a jam? Can He rely on you to pray with someone in need at any place and time? Are you embarrassed to be a Christian? Prioritize and grow. God hasn't given us a spirit of fear but of a sound mind. He will guard you and guide you. Your apprehension isn't from God. Be available. Don't hide from Him when He needs you most. He's using you to touch someone's life. You may be the last opportunity someone has to know God before slipping into eternity. Take the opportunity.

Challenge: God will find you. Seek Him every single day. Grow your spiritual life. Listen.

The happiest place you can be is in the will of God. Get there.

When I get frustrated or nervous, I find my happy place. We all have one. It's that place you mentally retreat to when you feel overwhelmed or anxious. Just a simple visualization can change the whole outlook of a bad situation. My happy place takes me back to a time when I was about six years old. I'm standing in the back field of the house I grew up in. The snowflakes are gently falling on the weeds and underbrush that dare stand tall in the wintertime. It's chilly. The temperature is so cold that I feel my cheeks getting frosty. My little woven mittens are no match for the chill in the air. I have on little snow boots to protect my feet. I can hear the crunch of the snow as I slowly walk around making patterns. My hat is neatly tucked down over my ears. I'm warm. I'm comfortable with listening to the cars drive by on the highway adjacent to the property. The soft sounds relax me as I listen to the howl of the air and watch the snow blow in circles near the ground. I look up at the sky and hold out my tongue to catch a snowflake. I'm protected. I smile. I'm relaxed.

Did you get the visual? Did you hear the sounds of new fallen snow? Can you see it with me? I love it there. I loved being little with no worries. I was safe. I was well cared for. I had everything I needed. Life was good. Sometimes, I have to retreat there for a while to regroup. I just stand and look around. I just watch and listen. It's where I need to be when I need to feel joy and happiness. The great thing is, I can go there anytime I need to. I carry it with me everywhere I go. It's always available and accessible. I lose myself.

When we have a place to retreat to, that means we have a reason to retreat. Going to your happy place doesn't mean you stay there forever. It's like a quick stay. In the chaotic world we live in, we have to be able to rest and retreat someplace to fill our emotional bucket. When we are constantly giving and pouring out ourselves to others, our bucket gets emptied. When we need a refill, we retreat to things to provide self-care. If we aren't good for ourselves, we can't be good for others. Sometimes, I'm around individuals who suck the life out of me. I can feel it draining my bucket quickly. I need a refill to be able to cope. I go to my happy place. Have you found one yet?

When we are in the will of God, we are in a happy place. Every day is new. I have been through situations where I just waited for the next good thing God was going to do for me. It was fun! I was in the will of God. I had made life changes under God's direction, so He was continuously blessing everything around me. My stress was abated, and I felt like I was walking on air. God took care of me.

I have also been out of the will of God. The unmeasurable amount of anxiety and hurt that I dealt with should have been enough to snap me quickly back in line. I continued out of the will of God. I was engaged to marry a young man. Even though he had completed drug and alcohol rehabilitation, I had some doubts about the stability of his life and my future. I was always on edge and felt more tense about the situation than happy to be planning to get married. Eventually, his drug habit came back. I called everything off. I was released from the heaviness of the situation like a load had been lifted off me. I retreated to the will of God.

I've seen individuals struggle with finding their place in the will of God. I've prayed with people to find their calling and position for God. It's not something that anyone can tell you; you have to find it on your own. You have to listen to God and be in tune with how your life meshes with God. The Holy Spirit will guide you; God will place you. We have to be willing to get away from pleasing others around us or doing what feels good and get back to what God wants for us. Pray. Ask God. He will let you know. He will guide you. You have to be willing to listen and do what He asks. Get your directions and be happy.

Challenge: Find your happy place. Find the will of God for your life. Be obedient.

People lose control of you when God gains control. Trying to please others stunts our spiritual growth.

Life would be much easier if we could just be ourselves and not have to worry about what people thought of us. We live in a society where peer pressure is real and bullying most certainly exists. Our world has changed into the most influential people gaining the most control of our lives. What we used to see as our individual freedoms are slowly being taken away. Money and power are the control factors.

Let's narrow that down to our Christian walk with God. Shouldn't we be able to walk into a church without the feeling of inadequacy in the house of God? Church should be a place of refuge and healing. It should be a place for readjusting and refreshing when we just feel spiritually beaten up. Yet Christians can be the most critical people on earth.

I remember my mom and dad getting into an argument about wedding rings. I don't remember my dad ever wearing one, but my mom did. At some point, she was told by a church member that women weren't allowed to wear rings or jewelry of any kind. I never understood the meaning behind it, but it had something to do with particular scripture in the Bible that had evidently been taken out of context. Later, the same church elders decided wearing wedding bands was okay to do. Wow, how times changed for the church.

I don't remember ever seeing my mom wear a pair of pants. I'm not sure if that had also been a religious guideline or if she just didn't like wearing them. She was okay with us wearing them. The church didn't allow for women to wear pants or anything that pertained to a man. That was a hard transition for me, since I was an outdoor kid and just didn't feel right in a dress.

Our church embodied a religion that controlled the people. Guidelines and doctrine were in place that kept everyone unified by their outward appearance, not their relationship with God. If you didn't agree with the doctrine of the church, you were welcomed to leave. They didn't want you to influence others in your beliefs. Members were identified by their outward appearance. They could be spotted anywhere in public. As we grew older, however, the church became more lax and loosened the restrictions on cutting hair and such. Those who didn't abide by the doctrine were rebels. Talk about your gossipers.

I'm saying this because I, too, was controlled by religion until I was in my thirties. At some point in my life, I realized that my outward appearance wasn't going to damn me to hell. I had a close relationship with God. After I gave up religion, I had an even closer relationship with God. Religion lost its grip on me, and God took control. In my efforts to please others, I lost sight of God. My spiritual life disintegrated. When I stopped worrying about what people thought of me or how I was going to disappoint someone by dressing differently, I flourished. I'm just sorry it took so many years off my life to figure it out.

I had difficulty understanding why the expectations set for me weren't the same for others. Why was it okay to believe that it was important not to wear jewelry or pants or cut my hair and then years later it was accepted? Why was my life controlled by others who couldn't even abide by their rules? It didn't make sense to me. When I realized that God wasn't in the mix, I escaped. My life had been controlled by others whom I desperately tried to please. Since my attention was on pleasing others, my spiritual life suffered. My relationship with God was superficial.

When God took over and gained control of my life, I was free. I learned self-care and how to express myself as a follower of Christ instead of a follower of religion. My life changed. God changed me.

Challenge: Evaluate who has control of your life. If it isn't God, change partners.

Any person can be a quitter. It takes a better person to persevere.

In my college psychology class, I learned that humans have a fight-or-flight response when confronted with danger. I would like to say that I am a fighter, but I have been known to be the flyer. I'm not one who dislikes confrontation, especially if I'm taking up for someone else. When I get angry, I have been known to walk away from a situation rather than say the incorrect words in the conversation. I avoid having to apologize, and I really dislike apologizing. When I get upset about something, I naturally shut down and walk away. It's my defense mechanism. When I calm down and can have a civil conversation, I do.

Growing up with my older brother taught me much about not being a quitter. I do remember him calling me names if I decided to quit on him in the middle of a game of basketball or football or whatever we were playing. He probably didn't notice that he was being mean, that he just wanted to harass me enough to make me persevere through the process. Coaches are like that too. That's why being on a team has benefits for building character. I was always one to please people, especially my coaches. I learned to get it done.

As a teacher, I try to build character in my students. I don't want them to give up. I want them to persevere through learning math or a concept in class. I want them to push through a challenging problem instead of giving up. I tell them all of the time to work through it and figure it out. In a way, I'm coaching them to do better for themselves. I want my words to ring in their ears as they move on to high school, life, and jobs. I am constantly giving them real-life situations of what would happen on a job if they were unprepared or didn't meet a deadline.

It's easy for me to relate to kids who play sports. I use analogies all of the time that they can relate to in their own lives. I want them to understand that if they learn to push through a difficult situation now, they will master it later in life. To finish, you can't be a quitter. Some kids still don't understand that they need money to survive in the real world. They are given everything they need. They don't understand the work ethic required to maintain a steady income and have what they want. They will understand later.

I wasn't much of a quitter, but it did happen. In those subject areas in school that were too challenging and stressful, I backed out. Sometimes, I just didn't get the importance of concepts. I had to understand why. I decided not to take classes that I knew would be overwhelming. I chose a profession that didn't require my challenging subject areas. I played it smart and lived within my means.

I remember quitting the basketball team in high school. I was going through a period of time when religion and church were overtaking my life and it was so very difficult to balance that and school activities. I loved playing basketball, and I was a starter on the team, but I was confused about life. The thing I loved doing, I chose to quit. Mostly, I quit because I knew I would make a greater godly impact. What I didn't realize was that I was letting people and friends down. God didn't care if I played basketball. Me quitting the team didn't help God impact anyone any more than I already was. I messed it all up, and I regretted it later.

We all face challenges. To persevere through the challenges teaches us valuable lessons. It's easy to give up and quit altogether. Pushing through a difficult situation builds character. We build self-confidence. We do it for others but realize that we are impacting our own lives. Success takes work. Sometimes, it takes long periods of time to achieve our goals. We can't give up. Our spiritual journey is the same. Sometimes, we have to push through spiritual battles to overcome our own insecurities and be successful. Don't give up. God didn't and won't give up on us. Push through until you see victory.

Challenge: Don't quit. Challenges build us up instead of tearing us down. Meet them head-on with God.

Standing alone isn't what it appears. You have a heavenly host assigned to you. If only you could see them.

We've all been there. You're at the bottom looking up; and no one is around to care, listen, or even bail you out. You feel helpless and alone. No one understands. Those who you thought would be there aren't there. It's as if the going got tough and the tough left you to fend for yourself. The only thing that sustains you is God.

I remember being at my darkest hour and spilling my guts to those who I thought truly cared for me. Instead, I received a lecture on how I should pray about my situation and give it to God, I was the one in the wrong and I needed to get my heart right, and I was at fault and needed to fix it. My heart was broken into pieces. I thought I was losing my mind. I knew I hadn't been at fault. My emotions had been trampled on.

So how did I handle it? To save face, I brushed myself off, prayed for God to help, and went on my way. Not receiving emotional support and backing caused mistrust and created a distance. I thought that if anyone would hurt me, I would leave before they had the chance. I was in fight-or-flight mode. Usually, I fled. I wasn't very confrontational, because I thought it was ungodly. I bottled up my emotions and shoved them farther and farther inside where no one could touch them. Eventually, they had to be released.

I saw how others were consoled and supported in times of need; I just didn't get the same treatment. I couldn't wrap my head around it. I saw how immediate comfort and reassurance went to certain individuals, but I was kept at a distance to fend for myself. I was truly alone with God. Even with God, I felt like I was trudging through mud to exist every day. I was actually going through depression and didn't know it.

God is always with me. I can't count a time where He didn't walk beside me, in front of me, or behind me in support. I never gave Him credit, because I was looking for human support and comfort. All the while, He was there. Many times, He carried me. When I was alone, I fell apart. God knew my heart. God understood. I didn't realize how much He cared until later in life. He had my back all the time. I pictured an army just waiting to rush to rescue me.

Jesus was alone many times too. He chose to be alone so that He could be with His father. I believe that He needed to feel renewed and refreshed away from the crowds. He was alone on the Cross. God had to look away at what transpired in the world and the loss that He suffered at the hands of those He created. Jesus could have called thousands to rescue Him. He chose the position to die for us. That was His purpose.

God has an army ready to rescue us at a single moment. God has our back. If only we could see what He has at His disposal to save us, we would never doubt again. We are not alone. Think about the times when you thought you weren't going to make it. God was there. Think about times when you had to make difficult decisions. God was there. He was your support. God could have unleashed a legion of angels to fight for you, but He waited. They're standing at attention. If He thinks you're going under, He rescues you with an army.

Depending on God instead of those who you thought were your friends makes a big difference. God tells us not to worry. He works everything out for our good. Sometimes, He carries us until we gain our strength. He's waiting for you to ask. He's standing at attention with an army. When you think you can't take anymore, He steps in. He won't put on you more than you are able to bear. Picture an army behind you. That should ease your mind pretty quickly. You're not alone. You have an army on your side.

Challenge: When you feel alone, ask God for help. He's there waiting. You're not alone.

It doesn't matter how many times you fall down. What really matters is how many times you get back up.

How many times in your life have you been told, "Get back up and try it again"? It's a common phrase. It tells us we can fall down or make mistakes but not give up. Falling down doesn't necessarily mean literally falling down; it's a term used to describe our mood or disposition as well. Our human nature allows for us to go through disappointments in our life in order to build ourselves back up. It's sort of like building up a resistance to the things that hurt us. Fighting through a bad situation heals us.

Growing up in a small rural town, I had the opportunity to be around farm animals. We had a few acres of land outside of town—enough room that my dad and brothers used to keep and raise different kinds of animals for food. My brother always loved horses, so we had those too. Riding was so much fun. I learned how to ride, groom, and even break horses because of my brother. He began teaching me when I was just a little kid. He also raised honeybees, but I didn't respond very well to that adventure. Eventually, my brother built a house a little distance away but had lots of land to raise horses and other livestock. He knew so much about animals even though he hadn't gone to school for any of it. It was so natural to him. Since his sons, my nephews, were about the same age as me, we were always riding the horses and playing out in the woods. Since I had school through the week, I would go to my brother's house on Sundays and hang out on the farm.

My nephew and I went riding around the property one Sunday afternoon as we usually did. I remember we were in the front lot away from the barn and started to make our way back. There was a dry creek bed with steep sides leading down to it. I didn't think anything of it as we started down the one side on the horses. My nephew was in front of me, so he didn't see what happened. As the horse got to the bottom of the creek bed, he quickly jumped to begin the climb up the other side. I wasn't expecting it.

I remember the horse lunging forward and me going the other way, backward. It wasn't the animal's fault; he was doing his thing.

I neglected to lean into the horse as it jumped, so the quick action threw me off his back. That's where I landed, on my back. It was a rocky landing. I was scraped up a bit and took the brunt of the fall to my back. Stunned and surprised, I slowly sat up checking that everything was intact.

Nothing was broken. The horse was nowhere to be seen. He kept on moving to the barn. Fear kicked in. Since I thought the horse had thrown me off, I was afraid to go anywhere near him. I knew what I had to do. I walked to the barn where my nephew was waiting. He told me I had to get back on the horse so that it knew I wasn't afraid and still in charge. Hesitantly, I did. Everything was good. It never stopped me.

When we spiritually fall down, no matter what the situation, we have to learn to pick ourselves up and go on. It's not an ego thing; it's more of a power builder. If we choose to stay in a depressed state, we're only hurting ourselves. No one can pull us out except ourselves. We have to want to do it. It's necessary to get back in the race and stay focused on our journey. The more times we jump back up, the easier it gets.

If we don't go through challenging situations, we never learn to rely on and trust in God. If we don't get knocked down once in a while, we lose sight of our purpose. We're not always going to be at the top and in our best game as we go through life. God is growing us through situations. We can choose to stay down, but the longer it takes to respond, the longer it takes to bounce back up. We choose the solution. Don't let someone or something take life out of you. You have a lot to live for. Just live.

Challenge: Reflect on the times you fell down. Think about how you recovered. Those are guideposts.

You may not know how you touched someone's life until years later. You may have introduced them to God.

When I was about fifteen years old, our church voted in a new and young pastoral family. They were not like what I had grown up with. It was a welcomed change. They were young, so they could relate more to the kids and young adults in the congregation. They were enthusiastic about the ministry and building up the congregation in our small town. Not long after they came, they decided to start a bus ministry. The purpose was to bring in kids for Sunday school so they could learn about Jesus. I was all for it. Having kids around seemed like it would also draw in the families. It was a good plan.

I enthusiastically jumped on board. It was a new experience for me, but I learned very quickly how to build relationships and not be afraid of inviting people to church. It worked! We soon had our refurbished school bus filling up and headed to Sunday school. This, too, added to my Sunday morning duties. I didn't mind, because I enjoyed hanging out with these kids. I rode the bus to pick the kids up for the morning service. I taught them in Sunday school and then interacted with them and even taught them in Children's Church. I was a stable figure for at least a few hours on Sunday morning for them.

As this part of our church ministry grew, so did the need to reach out to surrounding cities to minister to kids. It was awesome! We increased our fleet to three buses and brought kids in from all over the area. God was blessing us. I visited each kid on Saturday to remind them of Sunday. I didn't mind, because I really enjoyed what I was doing. On Sunday morning, they were waiting for us to go to church.

On many occasions, kids wouldn't be ready, and I was helping them find their shoes and coats so they could get on the bus. Parents had forgotten to get them up. The kids wanted to come to church; so we waited on them, fed them, and loved on them all the way to Sunday school. They were like my own kids. I felt a responsibility to them. They loved me too. This was it every Sunday morning.

I worked in the bus ministry for many, many years. I met so many kids and families during that time. Many parents were introduced to Jesus through the kids and our efforts. We were so blessed. These kids learned about Jesus through Sunday school and the songs we sang in Children's Church. They were growing up in a loving environment that lasted for years. Some quit coming after a while because they were growing up. I knew we had planted a seed in them that would grow. They knew Jesus.

During this time, one of my special families was devastated by a tragic house fire. A little boy, Bobby, was unable to be rescued and died in the fire. It broke my heart. He was only about four years old. I attended his funeral and supported the rest of the family through this time. I wondered if Bobby told Jesus that He knew me because I had taken him to Sunday school. I thought about how I had this little guy for only a short period of time but had introduced him to Jesus, whom he now knew face-to-face.

Many years later, after I stopped volunteering in the bus ministry, I stopped in this little gas station in the next city. I was paying for my gas and items. The young lady behind the counter asked my name. I told her. She said that she recognized my face and that I used to pick her up on a big bus for Sunday school. She said she would never forget waiting for the bus on Sunday morning and having so much fun. She thanked me.

I left the little store almost in tears. We talked a little bit. She looked all grown up. I had introduced her to Jesus. I had made an impact on her life. She recognized me in a good way. I'm forever blessed.

Challenge: Don't be afraid to share your life with others. You're sharing Jesus. You're making an impact.

When you're going through the motions of being a Christian, step back and readjust your life.

One of the good things about growing up and serving in church is that they taught me how to perceive and understand those around me. I learned to keep my mouth shut and my ears open. Sometimes, what I heard was disappointing, but I learned to be cautious around certain individuals as well. I had those who really taught me to socially interact with others. I was a very shy kid growing up. To see me was to think that I was mad at the world. I had reasons to mistrust others because of traumatic personal issues, but I was also learning to interact with my surroundings.

I first started teaching in Sunday school and helping out in Children's Church when I was in my early teens. As a kid, I knew I wanted to be a teacher like my older sister. I enjoyed working with the younger kids and had a connection of trust with them almost immediately. A small group in a class wasn't too bad to deal with, so I gave it all I had. I prepared my lessons and activities and was ready for an hour of power I needed to get through to these little angels. I quickly learned that little kids are a lot of work. I learned a lot of teaching skills and had awesome Sunday school teachers who showed me the way.

I knew lots of stories from the Bible because I had participated in classes most of my life up until then. I had my little lesson guide and a flannelgraph board for visuals. I actually became pretty good at my position. Eventually, I moved around to different age groups, so I learned to deal with all sorts of situations. I had kids in my class who had ADHD before it was even a diagnosis. I enjoyed teaching.

I graduated to teaching Children's Church on occasion. We had two age levels with about eighty-plus kids attending. I was helping out with the older group. Every weekend, I was teaching Sunday school and then helping with Children's Church. I wasn't being fed much on a Sunday morning. There were many times that I was absolutely exhausted after giving of myself for two-plus hours. I wondered why I was even going to Sunday morning service. I was becoming burned out. By the time the evening service rolled around, I was so tired and exhausted that I really couldn't enjoy it. I was going through the motions of being a Christian.

I was learning a lot. I was honing my skills that would become my future career but not looking forward to the weekends and Sunday morning duties. I enjoyed seeing the kids, but I was losing focus on God. This happened many times in my life where I was serving so much in church that I had to take a step back, take a break, and refill my spiritual life. I loved being in church but was exhausted all the time. I smiled and acted like I was okay, but inside the struggle was real. I didn't think God could be that demanding of me. He wasn't, but people were. If there was something that needed done, I was the first to volunteer. I had to regroup.

Going to church became a motion and a duty to me. I had a reputation to uphold because of being in the choir and holding so many jobs at the church. I felt I had justified myself by showing up and proving that I was faithful. People had no clue that I was absolutely exhausted, and it took everything within me to get through the doors. When I wanted to take a break, people thought I was losing God and backsliding. If I missed a service, I was called to make sure I was okay. No one took notice that I needed a break. No one stepped in to say they would help or take over for a while. I had to do it myself.

Don't get to the point that you become an exhausted Christian just going through the motions. You have to step back from your duties so that you can be spiritually fed. Good spiritual leaders should see your struggle and help you. You don't need to be afraid to admit you need a break to refuel. Do it for yourself.

Challenge: God doesn't require us to serve to the point of exhaustion. Be careful that you're serving for the right reason and not being coerced into duty because of your giving heart.

If you don't fill yourself with goodness when you're spiritually empty, the bad can overtake you.

In my lifetime, I've had the opportunity to be in the presence of good Christians and bad Christians. There is a distinct difference. Some see themselves as good Christians when, in fact, they exude negativity. Being a good Christian, in my eyes, is one who truly loves God and is not afraid to let you know. I don't mean that they nag you about God; they truly love God to the point that they genuinely let God shine through them. They are positive, loving, giving, kind, and easy to talk with; and their life demonstrates it. They love worship.

A bad Christian, on the other hand, is someone who regularly attends church, gives in the offering, fights for a specific parking space and seat in the congregation, speaks negativity about anyone or anything, and gives the attitude that the church and God owes them something for showing up. In addition, they can be the ones who secretly bash the pastor, complain about the music, or don't offer to help out at church or donate their time. They cause disruptions and divisions while claiming it's the will of God. You know who those people are.

So having been raised in the church and seeing both examples, I chose to go the good route. At first, I was misled into thinking that church was a duty to be performed and that giving my time and money was going to get me a special reward in heaven. Then I grew up and figured things out on my own. All the while, I looked at my examples as role models. Was that truly what I wanted to be? When I sang to God, was I really supposed to look miserable? I chose no.

As I was working on growing spiritually through my teen-age years, I had a sense of which adults truly loved God and were good Christians and those who caused divisions but were in church every service. I saw these same people bless their pastor on the way out the door and bash the service on the way to the car. I had first-hand knowledge of disbelief in people who were supposed to be my Christian examples. It was confusing. God helped me sort it out. I wasn't in the position to ask questions, because I was just a kid.

I began filling my life with God and His goodness. I remember that I got to the point of loving to be in church because I loved the praise and worship. There were certain individuals I looked forward to seeing in the service. As a kid, when I was struggling with something, I hoped a good Christian would come and help me pray about things. I was loving God and truly understanding what my role in life was going to be. God was showing me things at a young age and molding me into a good Christian. I wanted God to be so visible in my life that I didn't have to talk about Him; I was an extension of Him.

Just as it happens, Christians can go through spiritual lulls or dips. It happened to me when I wondered where God was. He was teaching me lessons and building my faith through it all. During those times, however, I looked at things differently. I became a bad Christian where I complained and even bashed a few people. It's during those times that I should have begun filling my life with God instead of letting my spiritual tank go dry. I was like my negative role models. The bad had overtaken me. My willingness to serve became a duty. My heart wasn't in it. I was going through the routine. I let my guard down.

The time when you have more questions than answers is the time to draw close to God. That's when you need to surround yourself with goodness and positivity. Sing and dance before the Lord in worship and praise. Hang onto the last thread of hope. Fill yourself with goodness.

Challenge: Keep refilling your spiritual tank until it overflows. There is more good in your life than bad. You have to see it. Choose to be a good Christian and glorify God.

Every temptation starts with seeing something. That's the hook that lures you in.

I can honestly say that I've never smoked, drunk any alcoholic beverage, or tried drugs. I've been blessed in the sense that I was an athlete growing up and valued the condition of my body. Playing sports helped keep me in shape and have a desire to be healthy. It was a good way to stay away from things that truly harmed my body. In Sunday school, I had heard that my body was a temple and Jesus lived there. To me, if Jesus lived there, I had to keep it clean for Him.

When it comes to addictions, I really don't have any except for sneakers. In my closet, you will find over thirty different pairs. I love the different colors and how they feel. I love the smell of a good leather sneaker. Call me weird, but I'm easy to track down if I get lost in a store. You know where to find me. I'm pretty sure it's more of an obsession than an addiction. I honestly believe that because I only had one pair growing up, I felt the need to get all I wanted as an adult. So I did.

I have been fortunate to not grow up around the influence of drugs or alcohol in my family. My mom would never let it on the property. My dad used to roll his cigarettes and smoke, but he wasn't a chain smoker. So I was around it but taught against it, if that makes sense. I'm sure there were times when my brothers probably sneaked it onto the property, but my mother never found out. She was pretty strict.

I was introduced to marijuana for the first time in middle school. I had friends who smoked it all the time. During lunch recess, we would sit under a big tree on the back side of the playground, and they would light up. I was asked to participate but never touched it. I knew somehow my mother would find out and beat me to death. They didn't treat me differently because I didn't try it; they were still my friends. I wasn't addicted.

Even in high school, kids would hang out behind the building and smoke during breaks. I went out once in a while but never did anything. I was hanging with my friends. I didn't go out with my friends too much outside of school but always heard about their "adventures." They were having fun, and thankfully, no one ever got hurt. We lived in a small town, and there wasn't much else to do.

In reality, the temptation was there. Had I wanted to participate, I could have. Kids at my school even smoked in the bathrooms during school. That's an addiction, or it could have been boredom. Either way, the temptation, along with peer pressure, was the beginning of an addiction for some.

One of the worst temptations coming from the technology age has been pornography. Using a computer, it's easily accessible. Anything you want can be found on the World Wide Web. It's just like a drug or alcohol. It starts with the temptation and then moves into participation. It can lead to broken relationships, broken individuals, broken marriages, and such a devastating mistrust. The sad thing is that even kids can get their hands on it too. It's easy to kid yourself and think that you can back down once you give in. It certainly goes a lot further than that. Not until damage has been done is the effect real and it's an addiction.

People go through rehab for addictions. They get clean and meet up with their old friends, and there it is again. The temptation is back. One look is all it takes to get sucked back in. The hard part is removing yourself and access to the temptation. It takes a strong will and desire to stay clean and beat it. It can be done. I know many living testimonials. Is it easy? No, it's one of the hardest things to do. Surround yourself with positive people who are good influences in your life. Fill your life so full of God that nothing else fits.

Challenge: Recognize you have a problem, and admit it. Tell others and get help. Separate yourself from the temptation.

If God was first in your life and you had what you needed, you wouldn't have to take from others.

Growing up in a large family taught me that what's mine is yours and what's yours is mine. We didn't steal from each other, but we sure did borrow a lot of things without permission. Sometimes, they weren't returned. When I was young, I had one drawer for my clothes, not a closet, one drawer. All of my worldly possessions had to fit into one drawer. I'm sure you're understanding my dilemma. My drawer was open to be rummaged through whenever anyone felt like it. But so was everyone else's. We had no privacy.

Yes, I've witnessed fistfights and clothes being torn off individuals because items were "borrowed" without permission. I still have dreams that my sister steals my car. It doesn't matter that I have two or three in my dream; she takes it without permission. And in my dream, my mother does nothing about it. I may need therapy for that one.

That being said, we "shared" a lot of things. Did we need them? Probably at the time, I would say we did. I didn't have a job. My older siblings had things I needed. I never really stole anything from them. If it happened to be available, I was known to help myself. I was just a kid. I didn't think anything of it. Most of my valuable items were useless to others, anyway. I became a collector at a very young age.

As a teenager, I had a job mowing lawns. I earned some money and could actually buy some extra things. By then, most of my siblings had moved out, and I actually had my own room with a whole dresser of drawers and a closet. My needs were met. I had privacy, and my material things were safe.

I'm speaking about material things, but I want to emphasize that nonmaterial items can be stolen from others. Think about those who've had their livelihood taken away. Or how about someone who had their self-worth stripped away? Many times, it's easy to understand "Thou shalt not steal" material items, but I think it goes in a different direction. I've seen people steal other's happiness and joy. I've been a victim of stolen identity. And I don't mean my credit cards and identification.

When I was a teenager and young adult, I tried my hardest to please others and make them happy. At some point, I was sucked into a dependent relationship where I felt like my worth and devotion were to other individuals and that my own well-being didn't matter. I lost who I was because I was so wrapped up into what others wanted to make me. I couldn't measure up all the time and felt worthless most of those years. I was made to feel that I was in the wrong if I had emotions or feelings that contradicted their positive happiness. Basically, I was used. It took me years to gain myself back. I recovered after seeking mental health services.

Many times, I have witnessed a religious individual demean others because they didn't perform to certain standards. Many times, I have witnessed someone's joy being taken away because material things and religious beliefs mattered more than a close relationship with God. More than once, I have seen conflicts in churches where people absolutely gave up and stopped coming to church altogether. Their relationship with God was compromised because others stole their joy and confidence. Yes, even Christians can steal from others.

When God gave this commandment to Moses, I'm sure there were things going on where it had to be said. How things have changed, and how perspective helps us understand that we can rob others in many different ways. We may not see it quite as clearly as that or write it off as a learning lesson, but it's stealing.

Challenge: Being a giver causes joy and peace. A thief lives in misery. Be a giver.

Hurting someone isn't always physical. You can mentally, spiritually, and emotionally damage a life.

I've had times in my life when I literally felt beaten down to the point where I lost all hope. Sometimes, it was from stress, sometimes from frustration, and sometimes at the hand of others. Sad to say, it was from those who should have been my role models, mentors, and Christians. Whether they thought it was for my own good or whatever lesson I was supposed to learn, it just mentally broke me. It was painful.

When I think about one of the greatest commandments to "not kill," I think about how humans can be oppressed in such a way that they die in spirit. Since the scripture doesn't say anything about murder in that passage, I believe it could pertain to an emotional death of someone. Think about how widespread abuse has become. It's not just physical; we're now dealing with mental, emotional, and spiritual abuses within our society as well.

On the flip side, how many of us have spiritually beaten down another individual because of our religious beliefs? How many of us have actually killed someone's spirit by beating them up with religion? It happens all the time. Growing up in a church where there were more "don'ts" than "dos" creates oppressive situations and crippling emotions. When someone is so driven by their religious beliefs where God is not the focus, it spiritually scars individuals for life when they can't measure up to the expectations.

Being a victim of spiritual, mental, or emotional abuse can take years of therapy and healing in order to sort everything out. God is not the author of religion. Man has taken on the role of interpreting the Bible into a belief system that they use to guide their spirituality. That's why there are so many different religions. The interpretation is perceived in so many different ways. Sometimes, God is lost in the translation.

Our beliefs, based on God's word, guide us through our spiritual journey. When our focus is on God, then our freedom to share God's word and love is pretty easy to do. If we truly share God's love, then those around us should prosper and grow. They, too, keep sharing God. God continues to grow in numbers. We see God moves around us and wants to do good for those around us.

If we choose to hold our religious expectations so high that others are offended or feel like less of a Christian, then it borders on a beatdown. We aren't growing God; we're killing others. I've often wondered why so many in my church decided to walk away from religion when they became adults. Was it the oppression and expectations? Was it because their spirit journey had been sabotaged by religion? What about those who are beaten down mentally and emotionally, and are trying to find rest in a church. Then they are killed by religion. It's spiritual murder.

Being a victim of spiritual oppression has helped me understand how to deal with people when it comes to God and my Christian beliefs. Isn't the most important thing in God's message to love others? We get so sucked into others' belief systems that we can't walk away but still keep hanging in there to get spiritually abused over and over again. Breaking the cycle frees us and heals us. God is our refuge.

Don't damage others because of how you believe. If you're truly a Christian, you should be loving others and keeping God first. Listen to that command "Thou shalt not kill" when you see someone in need. We can spiritually murder those around us because we think we're always right and holier than them. That's not God's intention. Love others. Be a guide. Be a spiritual leader that focuses on God and His word.

Challenge: Dig into God's word so you know and understand how to help others. Use it to guide you in your spiritual journey.

When you speak the name of God, it gets His attention. He's ready to listen.

I have often read product labels and wondered about some of the warnings that are listed on the product. Evidently, someone at some time has used the product for unintended use, and it was reported to the manufacturer. So in response, the labels are printed with warnings about unintended use of the product. I just shake my head in disbelief knowing that someone did such a thing.

When God gave the commandment to the children of Israel, He specifically stated that "they shall not take the name of the Lord their God in vain." Basically, don't misuse God's name, because He will not let you go unpunished if you do. So if God had to bring that to their attention, it must have been happening a lot. I believe that every time someone says, "God," He hears it and thinks they're talking to Him.

Growing up, we never used God's name except to pray. If used otherwise, a swift slap or scolding occurred. We learned quickly not to disrespect the name of God. I grew up with the thought that if I did say God's name and I wasn't praying or talking with Him, I would keel over dead immediately or lightning would strike me on the spot. I don't know why I thought that, but somehow it was in my head.

I remember standing at my locker in high school, getting my books out, and being very frustrated about something. I said, "God," out of frustration. I literally looked upward thinking lightning was coming at me right there and then. Nothing happened. I remember quickly praying and asking for forgiveness because I felt so guilty. I learned not to do that again. I survived.

To me, using the name of God in vain means that it is just another casual word. Being said casually means that all respect is lost for the true meaning of the word *God* for our Father in heaven. When it becomes just another byword, we have lost the value of who God is. God, Himself, in my opinion, is the one true God. There are many gods presented to us in this world. There are many religions that claim other gods as their saviors and helpers.

I can honestly say that I don't value any other god like my Heavenly Father. I don't acknowledge any other god around me. I don't trust any other god to take care of me and help me through my life except for God. I know from my personal experience that God is real. He's interactive. I feel His love and care for me. I honestly don't know how I would survive without knowing and trusting God.

I often wonder how people get through life without knowing God. Maybe they value other things to get them through their life and have sustainability to make it on their own. I'm not quite there yet. I can't imagine going through my day not thanking God or admiring His beauty all around me. I live in a world He created. I've seen miracles that only He could have done. I know He's real.

God gives me hope. If I didn't have something to believe in, I would surely be a mess. When I think of the goodness of God and His mercy, I can't imagine living my life without Him. So when I hear others use God's name in vain, it bothers me. I understand that they don't value God the way I do, and that's okay for them. I believe that at some point, though, they will need to call out His name and mean it. Many people meet God for the first time through tragedy or even near death. That's okay, too, as long as they meet Him.

I can't imagine going through this life and living in this world without God. He is my stability in all of the unrest. When I call on the name of the Lord my God, it's reverent and honorable. That's my God.

Challenge: Check yourself. When you speak the name of God, is it out of respect and admiration?

When you try to carve out a place for God in your life, that means you don't have time for Him.

If you had to choose between your worldly possessions or God, would you choose the worldly possessions? If you had to choose between life and denying God, would you choose life? Believe it or not, many have given their lives for the gospel and the one true God. How is it possible that some have such a devotion to Him and would give their own life and yet there are others who buckle under peer pressure and deny Him? Currently, in many other countries, there are those Christians meeting in secret and risking their lives because they truly love God and the Bible.

Growing up, I would hear stories about missionaries in other countries who were risking their lives to spread the word of God. As a kid, I couldn't imagine what it would be like to be in that position. I had my whole life in front of me. I thought about being held at gunpoint and given the choice to deny God and live or accept God and die. Could I really do it? Well, it scared me as a kid. As an adult, I would find it easy to make a choice. God has given me everything. Since I'm promised life eternal, what does this world matter?

The second commandment to the children of Israel was to not bow down to any other god or idol except for God. Remember that these people had fallen away from God and slipped into some idol worship, I'm sure, by living around the Egyptians. Their lives were full of pagan worship. It rubbed off on the people because they had taken their eyes off God. They had become more materialistic than spiritually trusting that God would take care of them. They lost focus.

Here again, God was placed on hold while the children of Israel meddled with the pagan worship in Egypt. They had even forgotten about the feasts and special events that they used to honor God. Each event had a particular meaning to remember from where God had brought them. I'm sure they had heard their forefathers talk about the blessings and goodness God had bestowed on them, but did they really believe it? The same people were the ones who wanted to go back into bondage just so they wouldn't have to travel through the desert.

Bowing down to someone or something means that you are under subjection and totally obedient to whatever or whoever it is. Over the years, I've been fascinated by the true stories of how individuals have been sucked into cult activity. A leader, who usually proclaims himself as God, influences vulnerable individuals into believing that they really are. People worship the leader. The leader demands worship and praise. People sacrifice themselves for false teachings and even harm others for the sake of the false religion. It blows my mind that individuals can be so caught up into lies and deceit from one individual.

We read about the tragic ends or see horrible pictures of devastation caused by idol worship and subjection to false teachings. The Word of God can be twisted in so many ways to deceive others into false hope and ritualistic thinking. Submission to someone proclaiming Christianity but requiring idol worship and dedication will most likely end in tragedy. Don't be alarmed, but there are false religions happening all around us even now.

God is so, so good to us. He deserves to be honored and revered. He deserves our obedience for all that He's done for us. His actions and intentions haven't changed over time. He truly loves and cares for us. He is the same yesterday, today, and forever. The same words that he spoke to the children of Israel are still being spoken today. God deserves our praise. We can gladly bow in submission. He knows our hearts.

Challenge: Remove those things from your life that you bow to. Your submission and obedience to things other than God tell the story. Get your focus back on Him.

You become generous before you become rich.

When you ask people what makes them rich, usually they refer to money and tangible wealth. When you ask someone who truly believes in God what makes them rich, it's usually spiritual. By spiritual, I mean the peace of God. It can be the blessings in your life. It can even be your family or your job or your health. Believing in God takes us to another level of wealth. We are blessed and rich because everything we have belongs to God and He has given us everything we have. It's a difficult concept for those who don't believe and trust in God to grasp.

Growing up in a pretty full household, there were many mouths to feed and necessities to take care of. I am the youngest of seventeen kids. Both of my parents had eighth-grade education. To see them manage a household was amazing for how young they were when they decided to get married and start a family.

To others, we probably fell into the middle class and maybe even lower. We were so very well taken care of in the sense that we had food, clothes, a nice house, and parents who encouraged us to attend school. They managed their money very well and even stepped out on business ventures. I believe they did the best they could, and to me, we were wealthy.

Our wealth came from the blessings we had every single day. My parents were in good health, as were all of us. We had nice cars to drive, and we had plenty of room to house us comfortably. What we lacked was somehow taken care of. We celebrated birthdays, Thanksgiving, and Christmas by having huge meals and a large portion of the family home together. We were rich in love and care for one another.

We grew up in a Christian home where we truly thanked God for what we had. We blessed our meals and thanked God that we had meat on the table every single meal. We were blessed that my dad raised huge gardens every single year to be able to keep us in vegetables, jams, jellies, and soup. I don't know how they did it, but they did. They trusted God to meet the needs, and He did.

With all that we had, I can remember that if anyone was in need, they were never turned away. When the church needed something, my mom was one of the first to donate and help out. She was very generous to the ministry of the church and work of God. She supported missionaries and evangelists who came through our small town. Seeing that made me realize that we had to be rich in order to keep giving away. As a kid, I knew what it was like to be generous and giving because my parents had modeled it for me.

Growing up, all I knew was to give. I gave my time to the church. I sponsored kids in other countries to help them receive an education and learn about God. When I started working, I gave faithfully to the church. I supported the ministers and housed evangelists who came through to preach. I gave unconditionally of my time and love to my students. Sometimes, I bought Christmas presents for my kids who had little. My family would sponsor them too. When there was a need, we took care of it. Our family lacked for nothing.

God was and still is the reason for my spiritual wealth and everything else I am blessed with. Nothing is mine. Giving generously taught me that I am very rich. I am blessed beyond measure because everything I own belongs to God. Without Him, I am nothing and have nothing. I am wealthy and blessed because of God.

Challenge: See the needs of others, and give generously. God will multiply your blessings and wealth like never before. It may not always be monetary, but your blessings are all around you. Find them.

Don't let someone else's convictions dictate your life. You will always live under their shadow.

A conviction is a firmly held belief or opinion. The term itself can be used in many different ways to describe many different situations. You can have strong convictions about religion, politics, dating, marriage, or even education. At any rate, usually, you stand pretty firm in what you believe to be true. Trying to dissuade someone with a strong personal conviction can be almost impossible.

It's okay to have certain beliefs and opinions. We live in a free country where we can certainly exercise our rights and freedoms. We have friends who have opinions and beliefs that may not jive with our own. It doesn't mean that we ignore or degrade them if they don't believe the same way we do. We can agree to disagree. It happens all the time. Our society is made up of many different viewpoints about life. We learn to pick and choose what works best for us.

I believe that some of my own personal beliefs were developed by those around me. Those who influenced me the most surely helped in molding my outlook on life and myself. My spiritual convictions developed early on. By listening to sermons and being taught in Sunday school, I was developing my own views about God, the Bible, and church. At a very young age, I believed that life was pretty much black or white. There was no gray area when it came to religion.

When I was old enough to understand what it meant to be committed to religion, I joined my church. The bylaws were read to me, and I was asked if I would uphold those words. I agreed, and my life changed. Since I had grown up playing on sports teams, I knew what it meant to be a part of the "church team." The expectations were different from just going to church. There was more of a conviction of how I measured up to the adults who I thought were continuously watching my every move. In church services, I thought I had to be the last one praying at the altar just so people would see how humble I was.

I thought that the more I dedicated my life and time to the church, the closer I was to God. No one ever told me any differently.

I felt the conviction of being in church for every single event and participating in every single program that was going on. I wanted to prove that I truly was a good Christian. I quit wearing pants, cutting my hair, and even the basketball team that I loved playing on. I thought people would see my devotion as a dedication to God. It wasn't. I was dedicated to the church.

Those who influenced me used their convictions to guide me. I was so gullible that I allowed it to happen and was miserable most of the time. They made me feel guilty if I missed a single church service. If a job needed done, I was asked, knowing that I wouldn't say no. I was shamed about wearing pants and how it dishonored God. I was shamed into not cutting my hair. It grew, all right, but being a tomboy meant I didn't really know how to take care of it.

I felt like I was living under someone else's convictions. I felt oppressed by what my mentors said to me about how I should be living my life. I felt a weight on my shoulders larger than life. It was a constant mental battle about how I was disappointing others if I didn't do what I was told. I was so unhappy. So many times, I just wished I could crawl into a hole and die. What I thought was going to be my greatest spiritual awakening turned out to be a spiritual nightmare for fifteen years. No one was there to pull me out. I was dying inside, and no one cared. They let me go. Their convictions almost cost me my life. Thankfully, God rescued me. He knew my heart and intentions. He was always there for me. He was truly my Savior.

Challenge: Reevaluate your convictions. If they don't line up with peace of mind, they're not worth it.

Your will has to be strong enough to get you through a test. Don't give up.

When I read about the martyrs who suffered and died for the name of Jesus, I am so deeply touched by their will to be strong in their torment and torture. If they had not endured through the trial, the name of Jesus would have meant nothing to those around them. Their testimony would have been a joke. Instead, Jesus was honored, and God was glorified.

I remember my pastors teaching about being strong enough to stand up for the name of Jesus when I was little. As a child, though, I never thought I would be experiencing the things I did as an adult. To me, a test is a duration of something that challenges your faith. As an adult, I've had plenty of tests. Did I question God? Sure, I did. Did I wonder why He let me suffer? Yes, I did. Did I blame Him? You bet. Then I realized the reality of it all.

When I was sixteen years old, my dad suffered a stroke. It wasn't major but just enough to hospitalize him and worry the family. He was okay and only suffered some paralysis on the left side of his face. The man had never been ill his entire life. As a teenager, I didn't understand the impact it would have on my own life. What unfolded the next year was my test.

As a result of my dad's stroke, he found out that he had black lung, emphysema, bronchitis, and major respiratory issues. The doctor advised my parents to move to an arid climate where he could be more comfortable. I was in the middle of my junior year of high school. My parents decided to move to southern Ohio. What? That's not arid. And before I was finishing the most important years of high school? I was angry, confused, and depressed, and couldn't understand the reality of my mother's thinking. I didn't matter.

Luckily, my sister allowed me to live with her family to finish out my junior year. Then I was shipped off to southern Ohio. I hated it. I was stuck. I was most miserable. I began to hate my mother for upending my life. To me, there was nothing logical about the whole thing. I wanted to graduate from my high school with my friends I had known for eleven years. I saw no way out. I made everyone's life around me miserable also. I hated going to church. I hated my family. I was questioning why God had me in that position. I almost hated Him. In my eyes, everything was so unfair. On top of the TV was a plaque with the Serenity Prayer. I hated that too. It was a constant reminder of God. Why wasn't I getting what I wanted?

The summer passed, and I was adamant about not going to school in a strange place to finish out my last year of high school. My mother bribed me with everything if I would stay. She even told me that my dad would start going to church if I stayed. He didn't, so I didn't. My mother finally broke and shipped me back up north. Again, I was blessed to have sisters who loved me enough to let me live with them. I wasn't a bad kid; I was just hurt. I finished out my senior year, graduated from my hometown, and stayed as far away from southern Ohio as possible. I went on to college, held jobs, and was happy to be home.

My test wasn't as some are for others. Illnesses, death, diagnoses, and addictions can all bring on unwanted tests of our faith. If I had waited on God, I would have matured more, I'm sure. I didn't. It's so difficult to see the end when you're in the middle of a dilemma. It can be physical, mental, emotional, spiritual, or financial. It doesn't matter what it is; it is a test of faith. Can we hold on and trust God? Can we make the right decisions? Can we completely trust God that He will do us right? It's difficult to say yes and get out of His way while He works and builds us up. The important thing is to step aside for God.

Challenge: The testing of our faith allows us to grow. Don't give up. Let God carry you. Trust Him.

Never think that when you do something for God, it's a waste of time.

I grew up in a small Pentecostal church in a small town. Most people in town knew we were the "holy rollers" and sort of let us be. I didn't really understand why until many years later, and I was much older, that my religious beliefs were a little radical. I grew up learning that things were pretty black and white with no gray areas to be had. I either succeeded by joining the church or failed and felt that I couldn't measure up to what others thought of me. Many I grew up with fell away from the church because religion was such a big part of our spiritual journey.

As adults, many fell away from God because of the way He was presented to us as kids. God was the punisher and out to get us if we messed up. He really had a bad reputation. I believed I was on a straight path to hell if I went to the movie theater. I lived under a shroud of condemnation for most of my early years. As a kid, I was scared to death that Jesus was coming back in the rapture and I wasn't going to make it. I lived in fear that I couldn't measure up to the expectations of my church. I had nightmares because of religion.

Once I joined my church, I felt obligated to follow the "rules" set before me. I am a natural rule follower, so that wasn't a difficult task. My life began revolving around church and serving others. I felt it was my duty to do as many jobs in the church because my good works would make me a better person. If something had to be done and no one would volunteer, I did it out of obligation. The show had to go on. I had no personal life, so to speak, and my immediate family was put on hold in order to serve in church. I was exhausted from working multiple jobs all week and then doing church activities on the weekends. We had two services on Sundays. I dared not miss a service either, or else I was a sinner.

It wasn't all bad, except that my life was put on hold because of church. I was exhausted because of church. I lost personal relationships and family members because of the church. I was confused and misled to the point that I couldn't even find God in the midst of all I was doing. I continued to work in the church and perform tasks robotically. I was a natural at teaching, serving others, listening, and giving of my time to others. When I stood back and looked at all I was doing, I looked for God. Where was He?

Because my mind-set was so messed up, I continued methodically and attended to others. Since I was exhausted most of the time, I had a very hard time understanding what good I was even doing. My obligation had become a routine. Sure, I served, taught, and gave of myself to others; but I lost sight of God. He was there, just put aside as I tried to please others. He blessed me as I blessed others. Even the recognition I received didn't faze me. It was a duty.

I often call those times in my life the "Lost Years." I had truly substituted duty for God. I didn't think that anything I was doing even affected others. I came to realize much later in life that it did. Those kids whom I taught in Sunday school learned about God. Those kids who rode my bus to church every Sunday learned about God. The ones I loved, reached out to, and showed mercy knew about God. While I was floundering, God was doing a mighty work. I didn't know it at the time. He allowed me to see it later. My devotion to people, not the church, made an impact that will never go away. They knew God better than what I showed them. God took over when I was trying to find Him. Nothing I did was a waste of time. It was all for God's glory.

Challenge: Do good even when you know there's no reward. Don't give up when you feel overwhelmed. Let God shine through you. You never know which dark space He will penetrate because of you.

The name of a church means nothing as long as you are fed God's Word and you feel God's presence.

I grew up with schoolmates from different religious backgrounds. I didn't always understand their beliefs, but I surely respected them. I grew up with Baptist, Apostolic, Presbyterian, Methodist, Lutheran, Catholic, Brethren, Episcopalian, some I can't remember, and, of course, Pentecostals. For a small town, we had a church on every corner, or so it seemed. If you didn't go to church, you could be considered an outcast. We just kept to ourselves and faithfully practiced our beliefs. We never discussed politics or religion.

It was rare that we even asked each other to attend our churches because we already attended our own. Everyone sort of knew that. I remember asking my mom to go to the Baptist Church with my friend on a few occasions. It surely was different from growing up in a lively Pentecostal church. I had questions when I got home. When different churches in town would have Vacation Bible School, it didn't really matter what denomination you were. It was fun, and it kept us busy over the summer. Riding on a church bus was so much more fun than riding on a school bus. In all reality, how are you going to convert a kid to a different religion in one service? Not going to happen.

I used to be scared if I did bring a guest to church or we had visitors at my church. I thought they wouldn't understand or respect my religious beliefs and maybe embarrass me out in public around my friends. In reality, I felt a duty to invite people to church but afraid that they would walk out because of something happening in the service. It's hard to explain, and yet it never happened. I was respected for my beliefs.

With all of the names of the different churches we grew up with and the different religious beliefs, there should have been one focus in each and every service. It shouldn't have been about the number in attendance or how much offering was collected. It shouldn't have been about who drove the nicest cars to church or who dressed in the nicest clothes. It shouldn't have been about who was best known in the community and who was godlier than others. Our focus should have been on God. Every service should have been about the love of God. Every church should have opened their doors to anyone in the name of love, grace, and mercy of God.

Finding a good church to attend can be a little challenging. It's not all in the name, though. Attending a church service allows you to see what happens and get a feel for what you believe. If your focus is on God, you will find a place to be fed. God will lead you. If you attend a place and don't feel welcomed, loved, or fed the Word of God, you may not want to stay. Regardless of the name of the church, look for God inside. If He's not there, don't waste your time. If you don't feel God there, don't stick around. A church should reflect God and mostly God's love.

Sometimes, we have to get out of the stigma of religion and being bottlenecked into one way of believing in order to find God. A good pastor preaches and explains God's Word. He lives God's Word. He understands and studies God's Word. If he doesn't, it will reflect in the church and the people. Find a good church, regardless of the name, that welcomes God into the services and feeds you God's Word. You'll grow.

Challenge: Check your present situation. Are you being fed God's Word? Do you feel the presence of God in the service? If so, then invite others to join you. God will take care of the rest.

As Christians, we have nothing to lose, nothing to hide, and nothing to prove.

I grew up in a small town in northeast Ohio. I went to school with the same kids from first grade to twelfth. We all grew up together. The families in town knew each other. Many of us were related. We were raised by a village. I had a school family, my real family, and my church family. The neighborhoods were bonded, and families watched out for each other. Your reputation preceded you. Everyone in town knew your business. If you were in trouble at school, word got home to your parents before you did. Lesson learned.

My real family and my church family usually consisted of the same people. The church people knew me from birth, so I could say they were part of my extended family. We all had each other's backs. I learned to be a giver from a very early age. We always supported the church through finances and attendance. Every time the church doors were open, we were there. When I played sports and told my coaches that I couldn't make it to practice because I had to go to church, they respectfully understood.

As a teenager, I was coming into my own trying to realize who I was, where I fit into society, and most of all how to love God in front of my peers. My school family was nice. I had friends from all the cliques. I blended in well with every group. I never knew an enemy and always supported the outcasts. They were my true friends. I mostly kept my mouth shut and just let things happen. People had a tendency to gravitate toward me because I was a good listener and a true friend. I still had some things to sort out, though.

My religion called for more "don't" than "dos": "Don't hang out with non-Christians," "Don't wear pants," "Don't cut your hair," "Don't drink or smoke," "Don't go to movie theaters," "Don't attend school functions (especially prom) and sporting events." My duty to my religion stifled God. When I committed to the church, it was all or none. I thought I was doing the right thing. Since I was taught most of my life that life and people outside the walls of the church were untouchable, my life spiraled to a minimum. The changes I made were for religion and not for me. My school family respected my decision but really truly didn't understand.

At almost forty years old, I realized that God loved me. I have had a relationship with God since I was about eight years old. What I thought was *godly* was simply religion. The impact I wanted to have on people probably didn't exist because of my skewed reasons. I gave up sports and things I loved doing just to satisfy the church. I had never really been taught that God loved me. God was the punisher for wrong. He truly got a bad rap. My efforts to change for the good only caused bad in my life. I lived for years trying to find out where I fit and what my purpose in life was supposed to be.

If I had known as a teenager that God loved me so much, my life would have taken a different direction. I would not have relied on others so much for personal affirmation and acceptance. My focus would have truly been on a God who loves me unconditionally. Yes, I have screwed up in my lifetime, but God still loved me. I had nothing to prove to others except that "religion" can ruin a life. I had nothing to hide except the true love of God to anyone and everyone. I had nothing to lose except the sincere, true love of God.

My life was so bombarded with what others thought about me or how I could please others. I never really focused on God like I should have. I had no reason to be afraid or doubt; God had my back.

Challenge: Love unconditionally like God loves you. Be forgiving, gracious, and accepting of those who cross your path. God put them there for a reason.

You've been delayed for a reason. Be patient.

You wake up late on an important day when you have a serious meeting planned. You spill coffee on your clothes as you hurry out the door. You get into your car, but it's not starting. Your tire has a slow leak, and you're not sure if you can make it. The kids wake up late and miss the bus, and now you have to drive them to school. The dog decided that going out once before you left for work was not enough. You catch every single red light on the way to work. You get stuck behind a school bus making the route. Someone is driving twenty-five in a forty-five-mile-per-hour zone. Construction is going on again.

Just reading the list makes you anxious. You've been there. The delays are endless when you're in a hurry. These days, we are mostly always in a hurry to get somewhere or be somewhere on time. We strive to do better, but the delays catch us at just the right time. You can look at the delays two different ways. They can make you irritated and anxious, or they can help you survive. You get to choose the outcome.

In most situations, we naturally become irritated and anxious. This leads to a chain reaction toward others and causes more stress on us. While you're trying to text someone at the same time you're trying to make up time to your appointment, you lose focus. You rear-end someone or inadvertently cut someone off in traffic. Then they become angry at you and are now tailgating you to the point that you slam on your brakes just to show you're still in control. When you finally get to your destination, you're irritated and angry that you are now late, someone cut you off, and none of it was your fault.

It's difficult to see the positive side of being patient when you're delayed. Have you ever thought about the fact that you were delayed for a reason? You started to work a little late. Near your house, there's been a serious fatal car accident that could have possibly been you on a normal day. Those few minutes of delay spared your life. Waiting behind the bus on the way to work allowed you to miss an opportunity to run a red light and get a ticket. Money is tight, and you would have to sacrifice paying rent or buying something you need.

Did you ever think that God was trying to get your attention? Do you think maybe He caused a delay in your schedule so that He could dial you back in? Did you ever think that your life was spared because your time was delayed even a few minutes? Everything happens for a reason.

God needs you to be focused on what He has for you. I believe He has appointed times for you to meet and randomly help individuals. I believe that He puts individuals in your path who need your encouragement and love. That's not much to give but required as followers of Christ.

On the way out of church one Sunday, I saw a lady walking toward the main road. I asked her if she needed a ride. She asked which way I was headed. I told her I was going wherever she needed to be. She had taken a bus to church from a good distance away. I drove her home without hesitation. That was a divine appointment.

I'd been patiently waiting for someone in the grocery line to check out. All the lines were so long. The person was anxiously waiting for the total. It was apparent they were nervous about having enough money. It was someone in need. As she began putting back items, I gave her money. Another divine appointment.

The next time you experience a delay, be patient. God has an assignment for you. There's a reason something happened in a safe place. He has spared your life. Be thankful for the hesitation.

Challenge: Don't let a delay ruin your day. Look for an opportunity to do good. Be patient.

When you lose the news, your relationship with God gets better.

Think back to a day in history where you sat in front of the TV just waiting for current details of a major event. I clearly remember September eleventh. It happened suddenly. As the tragic details of the event unfolded, the only station to watch was the news. We were given minute-by-minute updates with all of the immediate media coverage. When the gunman stormed Sandy Hook Elementary, I was glued to the television. I couldn't walk away from the tragic event that unfolded and devastated our country. I sat and watched the news for hours just taking in all of the details.

Let's jump to a more current event, the worldwide pandemic. In the beginning, there were just a few reports on the news stations. As the tragic details unfolded in other countries, we watched and waited anxiously for more information to be revealed. How these people get the stories is amazing. We have real-life events happening right before our eyes in real time. People panicked. We waited for directions and information to safeguard ourselves. Stores were overrun with anxious shoppers trying to prepare for the worst. We watched the news for hours, if not days, just to be ready.

Our current situation allows us media outlets like never before. We are inundated with information. When I think back in time to when I was just a small kid growing up in the sixties, life was simple. We had three different stations to watch. We had to read the *TV Guide* to figure out when the different programs would be airing. The stations all signed off at eleven o'clock. Our lives weren't revolving around media coverage. We learned to amuse ourselves by playing outside or interacting with one another. We didn't have the barrage of news pouring out from current events. We had to read the paper.

Because we didn't have an inundation of media, we actually learned to communicate and relate to one another. We learned to solve problems and interact with manners and respect. We learned how to work out issues and use our imaginations. Mostly, we learned how to cope with life. Technology wasn't a thing; we had to read books. We honed our social skills and paid attention to tasks. We learned to focus on what was important. School and church were our social outlets. Our focus was intentional.

News and current events are important, but when they become too much, we have to learn to step back and shut it down. It's easy. Turn off the television. Shut down the computer. The world will keep spinning, and life will go on. Social media has us wrapped up too tightly where we become dependent on immediate stimulation and information. Relationships cease to exist. We've forgotten how to communicate with others face-to-face. We've lost the ability to read people and make eye contact.

How do you think God feels in all of this frenzy? He's been placed on the back burner. We don't take time to have a true relationship with Him. We have lost the ability to simply pray and communicate with our Father in heaven. We have become less focused on listening to His voice and waiting for a response. Our patience doesn't exist. Our expectations for Him are immediate; otherwise, we believe He's forgotten about us and walked away. God must be saddened by the state of the worldly affairs. We are supposed to be about His business. He waits for us with anticipation. He longs to hear our voice. He's patient, loving, and kind.

Walk away from the things that hold you captive. Angry events make angry people. We have enough hate in the world. Shut down the news. Beef up your prayer life. Fix your relationship with God. Learn to be patient in a hectic world. Don't be fixated on the news events. It can be depressing. Get back to God.

Challenge: Limit your airtime. How much time have you spent with God today? Level things out.

When you're called by God, you will succeed. When you're called by man, you're going to struggle.

Have you ever known those kinds of people who believe they can call someone into the ministry of God? I'm not sure where they thought they became equal to God to do His bidding and calling. Some say they have the gift or that God told them to tell someone their purpose. In my mind, I'm thinking, *If God took time to tell you what I should be doing, wouldn't He have taken time to tell me?*

I learned to be very careful of those who placed blessings or callings on my life. I always thought that if God wanted my attention, He would get it all by Himself. There are those, however, who listen to others tell them what they should be doing. Many times, they don't last in the ministry into which someone called them. I've seen them called and then struggle to fit a position in which they weren't meant to be.

Growing up in my church, we had this woman who was always telling young men that they were called into the ministry. I'm not sure how she knew it, but they actually listened to her. One young man was a drug user and alcoholic. He went to a Christian rehab facility and made it through the program several times. He was pushed forward as if he would fulfill his calling. He was even recommended by someone to pastor a small church near our little town. The last I heard, he had stolen money from the church and disappeared.

Another time, she told a man that he was called into the ministry. He was new to our church, but she jumped right on it. We didn't really know much about him. No one knew his background or history, yet he was permitted to take the pulpit and preach. My spirit didn't gel with what he was saying, and I didn't feel comfortable with him speaking. There was something about him that didn't sit right with my spirit.

I believe that when God calls us into a ministry, we are certain about the position. Sometimes, it takes years for us to accept what He has for us. We can be miserable until we decide to fulfill the request and begin our journey. God sees us through. We grow and find our place. God calls us, not someone speaking on behalf of God. It's very different if those who are known to be prophets of God speak prophetic words to individuals. It happened all the time in the Bible. When someone who is not a prophet or prophetess of God speaks to us, we should feel uncertainty in our spirit. If it's God, it will jive with the spirit of God within us.

Those called by God do great things because God has good intentions of where they will go. They will last a long time in their calling, and the fruits of their labor will be many. Are there those who are called by God and unsuccessful? Certainly. Do they fall because God let them down or because they let God down? Most certainly, they left their true calling and godly focus on their ministry. Pastors and Christian leaders are human. We forget that they are tempted and tried like us. If they choose to fall into temptation, they are walking away from what God expects them to do.

At the same time, pastors and Christian leaders have the same door to God as we do. They are, however, held to a higher standard as godly men and women. They can still be forgiven. Their position may change, but they still have the opportunity to change for the better through Jesus. They may acquire a tarnished reputation, but they are forgiven. God still loves them. God can still use them.

Be careful of someone who tells you what your future holds. Be wary of someone who calls you into a ministry. If God isn't in the mix, it may be a struggle. Don't blame God if you fail. He's not the one who put you into the position in the first place. Pray about where God needs you and what He wants you to do. He will surely let you know. If you don't receive His calling, He will get someone who will. The job will get done.

Challenge: If you're not happy in your current position, pray about it. God can move you somewhere else.

God helps you forgive those who spitefully hurt you. Forgiving them is healing for your heart.

Nothing is worse than someone who is nice to your face and then stabs you in the back. We've all been there. Individuals who need to feel empowered are the ones who want others to see how nice they are instead of how spiteful they can be. They live on the surface, and superficial gratification is what spurs them on in life. They want others to see their material wealth instead of how they use that God-given blessing to help others. Those are the kind of people you need to be wary of.

I've had the opportunity to live with materialistic people. It seems that even when they were showered with precious gifts, nothing was good enough for them. Individuals would bless them with expensive items that were bought on a shoestring budget. Yet they were scoffed at when the giver wasn't around. They were all about having the best and impressing those around them. Their image meant everything to them. They lived to please others. Their level of godly devotion wasn't deeply rooted.

It's easy to identify people who are wrapped up in themselves. And, yes, they are even found in the Christian body of believers. Sometimes, the vilest people can be the most avid church members. They love you to your face and speak ill of you behind your back. They gossip about others because they don't quite meet their standards or expectations. These precious church members are the first ones to reject those who are in need. They visit the sick and attend to the poor because it's their duty, not because of love.

I had the opportunity to be used by individuals whom I trusted to help guide me through my spiritual journey. When I thought that I meant something to them, I found out that I was being used. When they came into town on business, they would gladly stay at my house, eat my food, and use my facilities, but had not much else to do with me. They didn't even make the effort to take time to visit with me. They did, however, enjoy having people over at my house and taking time to visit with them while I was at work. I was heartbroken, but I gave them space. I'm guessing I learned a hard lesson in long-suffering.

At one point, I opened up my house for their friend to stay until an apartment came open. This wasn't my friend, but I did it out of respect to them. I thought that if I was nice and helpful, things would change. It didn't. I learned that the friend was just as insincere and superficial as they were. I was trying to hold onto a friendship that was dwindling away. Being nice got me nowhere. I had to learn to forgive.

Forgiveness is a very hard lesson to learn, especially when you know that you have been used. Jesus taught us that we are supposed to forgive others seventy times seven in a day if necessary. That's a lot of forgiveness going on. Having your kindness trampled on by uncaring people makes for a lot of hurt. Yet I had to forgive. Having people stay in my house for free yet disregard my feelings was hurtful. I had to forgive. I didn't forgive them for their sake but for mine. I lived in a world of guilt over something I had done when I hadn't. I had to learn to forgive myself too. I was a people pleaser, so I had a difficult time with the separation part and realizing that everything was not my fault.

People will be who they are. Christians will be who they are. I guess the greater expectation is that when we represent Jesus, we should be a little more caring and humbler. That's not always the case. We have to forgive Christians who spitefully use us too. Don't be put into a position where they're the victim and you're the one at fault. Things get twisted quickly. Get yourself out of situations where you're being victimized. Eventually, you will learn to forgive. Do it sincerely. You're clearing your heart and moving on.

Challenge: Pull yourself out of relationships that make you constantly forgive others. It's not your fault.

Being a morally good person doesn't excuse you from sin and being held accountable for your actions.

Have you ever met people who are just truly genuine embodiments of all things good? I have come across so many good humans in my lifetime. They are all about giving, helping, and encouraging; never have a cross word for anyone; love life; and enjoy every moment of the day. Yes, you know them. Sometimes they have wealth, and sometimes they have nothing. They have a stellar reputation that can't be refuted. They live an exemplary life that all around them admire and adore. They can do no wrong.

All good people don't necessarily go to heaven. The Bible tells us that it's appointed unto us to die humanly. After that what? We face God. Yes, we are held accountable for our life. The Lamb's Book of Life has our names written in it if we have asked Jesus into our lives and forgiveness for our sins. That's our heavenly ticket to eternity. It sounds so much like a fairy tale. Believing in God and His word makes it real.

The Bible tells us that after the Great Judgment, our fate is sealed. We pass on through either the pearly gates of heaven or the fiery gates of hell. There are basically two choices. Those who have had near-death experiences have explained both. Of course, the beauty of heaven is unimaginable. The torments of hell are beyond anything we've experienced in our lives, according to individuals who have experienced it. Imagine living either place for eternity. So think back to a morally good person who is expecting to die and go on to heaven. It may be disappointing to have done so many wonderful things in life, only to be living out the rest of his life in torment. Near-death experiences have caused individuals to not fear death or change their lives before it's too late.

Whether you believe in the Bible or not, it is the Word of God, inspired by Him as a guide for us who believe and follow. If you choose not to believe in the Bible as God's Word, you will still live life. You may still be a good moral person, but you eventually will meet God. Whether you believe in creation or some other gods, you will still live life, but eventually you will meet God. If you believe nothing about God or the Bible, eventually, you will meet Him. At some point, we will all recognize and honor God. Some of us choose to do it in our human lives.

Being raised in church doesn't necessarily mean that you're a good person and you're going to heaven. I have a brother who was in his later years when he finally met God. His granddaughter had been kicked in the head by a horse. She sustained injuries to the point where she had to be life-flighted to the hospital. She was about seven years old. The family all drove to the hospital to be with her and wait on the results. During that time, as the Christian believers prayed for my niece, my brother recognized that he didn't know how to pray. He was led in the prayer to ask Jesus into his life and forgiveness of his sins. Though he was a morally good person, he needed that final touch of Jesus in his life. His granddaughter fully recovered with no damage. He learned to talk with God and hasn't turned back.

Sometimes, God puts us into situations where we really get to know Him. It doesn't happen all of the time, but He knows when He needs to intervene. God doesn't want any of us to perish into an eternity of torment. He does give us opportunities throughout our life to make the choice. He gives us free will to choose. In the end, however, He has the final say. It just takes one time of asking Jesus into your life to receive heaven. It's part of God's plan. Don't let anyone scare you into becoming a believer. God knows you. He will draw you in. Until then, live a good moral life. Just be ready for the finish. Add Jesus. He's waiting.

Challenge: Check yourself. Have you asked Jesus into your life? Have you asked God to forgive you of your sins? Now is a great time to add heaven to your bucket list. Don't wait. You're missing out on so much.

Don't let the devil beat you up about stuff God has already forgiven.

I have learned that I am my worst enemy. I have the innate ability to be very hard on myself and hold high expectations in my personal life. I'm not sure where it came from. My dad was always telling us about doing jobs the right way the first time and not needing to go back and fix a mistake. He would remind us of giving our best effort at whatever we had to do. He didn't allow us to be slackers. We learned a solid work ethic from the time we were just little. My dad was a very hard worker and valued on job sites.

I say this because I have a difficult time forgiving myself. When I mess something up or inadvertently hurt someone's feelings, I am very hard on myself. I hate to apologize. When I say something that should have been filtered, I catch myself, but it's too late. The damage has been done. It's not easy for me to admit that I'm wrong. To me, that means failure. It's a difficult thing to live with.

God's grace has sustained me all my life. I don't take it lightly. Even though I have grace, I don't intentionally sin knowing that I will be forgiven. That's not the way grace works. I am held accountable for my actions. We are all held accountable for what we do. Some people believe that there is no sin because grace covers it all. The Bible tells us that we have all sinned and come short of the glory of God. We sin daily some way or another. We are capable of killing someone with our tongue. We are capable of killing someone in our thoughts by hating so viciously that it hurts our spiritual life.

The nice thing about God is that when He forgives us, it's immediate. He doesn't wait around to see if we really mean to be sorry or beg for forgiveness. We ask and He forgives. Our sins are thrown into a sea of forgetfulness. The problem is that sometimes we doubt if God forgave us. Sometimes, we ponder over our sin to the point where it can cause us to be sad or even depressed. It's not that because we are forgiven, we are to be totally joyful and then do it again. We have joy because our sin has been forgiven. Then we choose not to do it again. There is a difference.

Why can't we get to the point that when God forgives us, it's over? I believe it's because the devil keeps reminding us and has us doubting God's grace and mercy. He wants us to be miserable and find fault with God. He wants us to sin again and again and again. He wants us to believe that grace covers whatever we do, so why not go and have all the fun we want to since God said He would forgive us? The devil twists things to his advantage. If we are miserable, we're not our best for God. He likes it when we are depressed, fearful, and worried. He's not stupid. On the contrary, he was able to convince one-third of the angels in heaven that he was as good as God.

I ponder my mistakes and feel remorseful. We all should. God has higher expectations for us. He expects us to mess up once in a while. We're not perfect. That's why He provides a way out through grace. Jesus died on a cross and suffered death for all of our sins. He died for you and me, and we weren't even thought of back then. Because of His sacrifice, we are forgiven. Even better, we don't have to perform sacrifices to atone for our sins like in the Old Testament. Jesus was it. We have a direct line to God when we fail. He's just waiting.

When you mess up and sin, you have forgiveness from God. Don't let the devil beat you up day after day with what you did wrong. He likes to remind you so that he feels he's in control and has you under submission. You have to let him know that you are forgiven and God's got your back. He'll back down. Accept forgiveness and then let it go. Learn from your mistakes to be a better person. That's how you grow.

Challenge: When you are reminded of your wrongdoing, worship and praise God for forgiveness.

Changing your heart changes your tongue, which changes your words.

Have you ever been around those people who speak without a filter? You are thinking of someone right now. How do they make you feel? For me? I feel so uncomfortable and defensive as if I have to not encourage anything to come out of their mouth but also be ready to defend anyone on the receiving end of their words. It can happen in restaurants, in a store, out in the mall, or in any location available. Unfiltered people have no boundaries. I stand back and wonder, "Did you *not* just hear what came out of your mouth?"

Then there are those who speak straight to the point. My dad was a very reserved individual. Living with my mother and raising seventeen children, he probably just realized that he didn't have a chance to get words in edgewise. When he spoke, however, he meant what he said. He laughed at us a lot. When he spoke, his words spewed out wisdom that we still talk about today. He was so smart and self-taught.

Have you ever been around a Christian who lacks a filter? It seems that being a believer would automatically mean that love and encouragement drip from their lips. Yet there are those who still let their human side take over once in a while. We speak from our hearts. If what is falling from your tongue isn't pleasing to God, then it's time to readjust your heart. Does it mean that we always have to be serious? I don't think so. If we didn't have a sense of humor, then how would we draw people to God?

When Jesus comes into our lives, we truly have a spiritual change. I can remember being just a kid at eight years old and thinking that I was now representing God. I wanted to be a better person. I wanted to learn as much as I could about God. I wanted to know what Jesus's mission on earth was really all about. I wanted to be kind in what I said instead of hurtful. I learned the Bible scriptures and applied them to my life. I sang songs that touched my heart and drew me closer to God. Good came out of me.

God works on us from the inside out. God sees our heart, not our skin color. He created us all equal; that's why we have the same parts. God created a clean heart in all of us. We are born into a world of sin. We are human. It's our choice to welcome the spirit of God into our lives to help us be better individuals. If our hearts are bitter, dark, or even unforgiving, our tongue and words reflect it. We have the choice to change what is inside so that what comes out of us is pleasing to God.

We have the choice to speak life or death to others. As a teacher, I have 180 days each year to build up my students or tear them down. I have been put on check more than once because of being frustrated and disappointed. I never miss an opportunity to openly apologize for negativity that may have slipped out in a period of anger or impatience. My kids get enough negativity at home, sometimes, so I try to be the most positive that I can. When I have a difficult time saying nice things because my heart is hurt, I don't say much at all. My filter is on high alert. I've learned to keep my mouth shut more than once.

Every year, I ask the opinion of my students to help me be a better teacher or individual. I let them anonymously write their comments and be straight with me. Sometimes, they pick out my flaws right away. The comments never hurt my feelings, because I know that I may need an attitude adjustment to be better next time. Kids are brutally honest. I welcome their comments, though. I've been told I'm impatient. Yes, I can be. I've been told to be less sarcastic. They are not afraid to let me know. I love them for that.

This year was the first year that I wrote cards to each of them individually. I hope that my words of encouragement will forever ring in their ears. When my heart is right, my words are right.

Challenge: Think before you speak. Do you want to speak about life or death? Choose life.

How do you respond when God says nothing?

We've all been at a time in our life when we have waited on God. Sometimes, He answers us rapidly, but then sometimes He takes His time with the response. It's in those moments when we wait for what seems like forever for Him to get back to us. Did you ever wonder why He takes His time? He knows it all. He knows our need even before we ask. He knows what we're going to ask before we ask it. So why does He make us wait so long for a response? It's perplexing to me.

Questions usually get posed to God such as "Where were You when I needed You the most?" Or maybe "Why, God?" stumbles from our lips. I'm sure He's heard many. It's as if we have Him on a time line of expectation without realizing that He has our best interests at heart. Since He knows the outcome, there's no rush on His part to make a rash move. God hears our prayers. He knows our cries. He feels our pain. He sees our tears. Usually, the times we think the quickest responses from Him are needed are when we're in distress.

Why does God not respond quickly? Maybe He wants to build our faith. Or maybe He's teaching us lessons. Maybe He's growing us a little or stretching our spiritual boundaries. God doesn't really owe us anything. He provides for us and takes care of us in His own way and time. He truly knows what's best. He's our Father. He's not going to set us up for failure. Maybe He wants us to realize that our expectations aren't quite lined up with our needs. I believe God tries to balance our good with the bad.

What do we do while we wait on God to respond? We dig into His word. God guides us with scripture to heal our hearts or give us direction. We search for passages of scripture that comfort us and make sense to our circumstances. We pray. No, we really *pray*! We fervently and with all our hearts take our petitions to God. We dedicate time to talking with God and reminding Him of our situation. We ask for our faith to be built up and His will to be done. All the while, He is listening.

Waiting on God requires patience. We listen intently to that still small voice that guides us through our circumstances. We search for a light that pierces our darkest of nights. We pray. We talk with God and thank Him for the outcome that He already has prepared. We take time to focus on Him in the midst of our very busy lives. Our full attention rests on Him and His answer. We are more attentive to His voice so that we can make the right decision. Our spiritual ears are open more than ever. We wait.

God listens. He waits for us to be where He needs us to be. He knows where we're going and the plans He has for each of us. He's waiting for us to realize our own potential. He's growing us. He's taking us to places we don't even know yet. He's preparing us for journeys. He's getting us ready for battles. He's taking us to the war room. He waits.

When the time is right, God answers. Sometimes, we feel it's too late, and we question His timing. "If only You had been there, God." He was. Think about the situations that could have been much worse had He not been there holding you or keeping you safely away from harm. The easiest thing to do is turn our backs on God when the answers don't come soon enough. As humans, we need to have someone or something to blame. We choose to walk away from God, but He doesn't leave us. We choose to get angry at His decisions even though He knew what was best for us.

When God says nothing, it's for our good. It's never a punishment. He has plans for you that you don't realize yet. He's there. He's listening. He's waiting. He will answer. Dig in and find Him.

Challenge: Don't give up. When you wait on Him, wait. Pray. Be encouraged in scripture.

This life is temporary. We're headed home. There is more to what we're living for.

Growing up in a Pentecostal church, I heard hundreds of sermons in my lifetime about heaven and hell. I can't really remember the first time I ever heard about either place. I do remember that a description of *hell* was so scary to me as a kid that I knew I didn't want to end up there. Preachers have a way of scaring people into heaven. I was one. I've seen people run to the altar after hearing a fire-and-brimstone sermon about hell. The scare tactic worked. I believed then as I do now that both are real.

Heaven and hell are both mentioned in the Bible. They are referenced in several different places. I've heard stories of people who have had near-death experiences in both heaven and hell. I've read books that make them seem plausible to exist. Yet some people don't believe that either exists in the afterlife.

I remember being about fourteen years old and talking with my mom about the subject. I remember telling her that I thought I knew where heaven and hell were located. She asked my opinion. I remember telling her that heaven had to be so far away from us in the heavens. It exists where nothing else is. I told her that hell had to be in the center of earth where the hottest part of the planet is located. Since hell is supposed to be a place of fire, it made logical sense in the core of the earth.

Some people think that we are living heaven and hell here on earth. I have a difficult time understanding that logic. From the descriptions in the Bible, nothing here compares to either place. I believe that if that was true, nothing could be better or worse than it is now. I would have no hope in the promises of God and the truths that I've been told all my life. I would be living my life for nothing except the here and now. I know that more exist than what I'm living for right now. I feel it. My desire is heaven, not hell.

The sign of a good vacation is when you are ready to go home. You've had a time of rest, fun, relaxation, and peace; and you're revived! Going home isn't so bad. When I think of going to my heavenly home, I feel the same way. My race has been run. I have accomplished my work for God. I have done what I'm supposed to do. I feel content and fulfilled that my life has been worth something. I have a longing to be in heaven with those whom I miss.

I want to see Jesus. I want to be in God's presence where I don't have to do anything but relax and hang out. I will be free from earthly sorrows and burdens. I won't hurt any more physically, mentally, emotionally, or financially. I won't have any worries or cares. I'm not on a schedule or worried about my own well-being. I want to hang out with Peter and John. I want to talk with Moses and get his take on talking with God. I would love to sit down and listen to David tell of his victories and how much courage he had facing a giant! There are so many saints I would love to visit with. Mostly, I want to see my mom and dad again.

I heard that a sign of a true believer is a longing for heaven. We need to understand that this life is temporary. There is nothing here that is permanent for us. All we have, God has given to us. We exist to perpetuate the love of God and His goodness. When our time is done, we have another life to attend to. We choose where we want to go. It's pretty simple. We all will face God someday whether we believe in Him now or not. He's not a myth or a legend. Heaven and hell are both very real. It's not a fairy tale.

I believe that God allows us glimpses of heaven to stir our hearts and build our faith. If we saw it in all its glory, we would want to get there faster. I don't think we can imagine all that awaits us. I want to go. I long to be home. My book of life is quite full. I've accomplished a lot in my time. I'm ready. Are you?

Challenge: Take stock of your spiritual journey. Are you longing to be home? Do you miss heaven?

When you honor and thank God, don't worry what others think. He saved you, not them.

No one knows your story better than you. I remember as a young kid sitting in church and listening during testimony time. I would listen to the adults tell stories glorifying God. Story after story being told and not one the same as the other. Sometimes, my little heart was stirred to tell what God had done for me. Usually, it was a healing of some sort like a toothache or headache. Nothing was as exciting as what I heard others talk about, but it was *my* story. I was learning to openly tell of God's goodness and give Him honor.

As I grew older, my testimony changed. I was growing spiritually and learning my way, so I had real things to talk about like better opportunities or job changes. God was always recognized for His goodness. Since I didn't drink or smoke, my testimony wasn't as serious as some I had heard. In reality, I knew God saved me from many things, but they just didn't have the depth as those who had kicked addictions. I was in awe of near-death experiences and how God snatched someone's life from hell at the last minute. I told you they were dramatic. I believed every single person had their own story, so I never doubted any of it.

When you share your testimony, people rejoice with you. When you help someone understand where you've been, they relate to you better. When you hear someone tell of the lowest times in their life and how God saved them, you rejoice with them. You have a lot to share. When God truly does something amazing in your life, you want to tell others. It's not just a story; it's a miracle! All the world should know! It may not be anything spectacular, but it's important to you.

We all have different stories to tell. When I see a panhandler on the side of the street, I ask them what their story is. I want to know how they got to where they are. I want to offer resources to help them. They need help, but sometimes, they need someone to listen. Truly, they have a story to tell. Sometimes, I actually take their time by parking my car and talking with them to truly get the real picture and care. It's unbelievable at times. I can't imagine being in their situation.

When I'm in church, I worship God. I love being in His presence. I don't look around to see who's watching me. My heart gets so overjoyed that I can't stop the tears streaming down my face. No one needs to know what a good or bad week I had; they just know that I'm crying out to God. They may never know my story, but my emotions paint a picture for them. The depth of my spirit interacting with God shows the honor and glory to my Father, who has once again saved me. That's my testimony. No words are needed.

Our level of praise and honor to God comes from our innermost being. When we have experienced extreme hurt of pain, our spirit cries out in ways that we never imagined. When God blesses us with gifts that defy all odds, our spirit connects with God. No words are needed. Sometimes, the spirit of God intervenes on our behalf when we don't know what to say. God knows our heart. He feels our emotions. No words are needed. He knows our gratitude through our tears.

When others don't understand why you honor and worship God the way you do, they don't understand the level of gratitude you owe Him. Your praise comes from true humility and thankfulness for overcoming your circumstances. When you honor God, don't worry about what people think. It's *your* time to show God how truly grateful you are for His goodness and mercy. No words are needed. Be thankful.

Grow your testimony. Your words are more powerful than you think. Honor God anyway. Don't be intimidated by being thankful. God knows where you've been and what you've come through.

Challenge: Is your testimony honoring God? Share the good with others so they know God.

The closer you are to God, the more you enjoy His company. He's your Father. Give Him you.

When I was growing up, I was surrounded by family. Because I was the youngest and my parents were older, sometimes, I felt misplaced because of my nieces and nephews. In reality, we were pretty much the same age. We were more like brothers and sisters. I found it very hard to see my little nephews and nieces get all of the attention from my parents while I struggled and competed for their attention. I was jealous.

As a kid, I wanted my parents' attention and love. I wanted to be around them. Up until my feet were dragging the floor, I wanted to be held and rocked by my mom. I saw how sweet, cuddly, loving, and kind she was to the little kids, but I felt left out when they were around. Why didn't I matter? Why didn't my dad's eyes light up when I walked in the room like they did when the younger kids came over? As a kid, it was very difficult to understand. Since I didn't have younger siblings, I was experiencing loneliness with my younger nieces and nephews. I wanted attention. They didn't have enough to go around.

As I grew older, I required less attention. As a teenager, I didn't want their attention. I craved attention, and thank God I didn't misbehave to get it but learned to live without it. I enjoyed being around my family and had older siblings who gave me what I needed. They stepped in as my parents. Thankfully, I was more well-rounded than I realized. I survived.

Our spiritual relationship with God should be the same way. We should want to have such a close relationship with Him that we crave His attention. We should want to be rocked in His arms and held tightly when it hurts. We should want to make Him proud and value His opinion. We should want to be so much like Him that others love Him too and are jealous of us. God is our Heavenly Father. He is a jealous God. As much as we desire to have His attention, He desires our attention and time as well.

I find myself wanting to be close to Him. Just like wanting my parents' attention, I want to be in God's presence. I want Him to smile when He hears my name. I want Him to enjoy meeting me when I pray and talking with me about my day. I want Him to just be there for me when I'm hurting and give me advice in tough situations. I want Him to fix things so I can feel better. I want Him to give me wisdom and reassurance that things will be okay even at my darkest moments. These are qualities of a good parent.

As an adult, I'm not as needy as I was as a kid. I have learned to stand on my own two feet and grow spiritually to the point where I can ask God questions when I don't understand. I just simply want to spend time with Him. I find myself talking with Him throughout my day. I love thanking Him for the beauty all around me and my blessings in life. I laugh with Him and hope He understands my humor and wit. I want Him to be so proud of me as I walk my journey through life.

Both of my parents have passed into eternity. Sometimes, I still crave their attention and want to make them proud of me. I'm different from who I was when they were around. I've grown more and come into my own. I've succeeded in ways that I never thought I would. Just to hear them say they are proud of me would mean the world to me. I miss my quality time with them, especially my mom. There are so many things I want to tell them. I would love to just sit down and have another conversation. I miss them both.

With God, I always have my Father. I draw close to Him because I really enjoy His company. He's a big part of my life. Keeping an open communication helps me stay in His presence where I need to be. Draw close to God, and He will draw close to you. He doesn't ask or expect anything but your attention.

Challenge: Measure the distance between you and God. Could you be closer? Give Him you.

Don't measure your fellowship with God based on what you see in others. Be yourself. You're unique.

Have you ever just sat in church and watched people? It can be enlightening. People worship God differently. People sing to God differently. People even pray differently. It's not that they usually do anything to draw attention to themselves; they just naturally have a love for God in what they're doing. You can almost see God right there with them. They are so enthralled with and focused on God that you just want to stand next to them and enjoy the blessing. They emit a presence that is so enticing. I want to be like them!

I have had the opportunity to watch my church online since the pandemic, but it's nothing like being in the church building in corporate worship with other believers. There's a certain feeling when you have a purpose for being in church. Your mind is focused on God, and you sing from your heart. You've had a tough week, and just being in the church offers peace and comfort for some reason. Being around others who truly love and worship freely is encouraging.

I have had people come to me after church and tell me that they enjoyed watching me in the worship service. I wasn't doing anything special; I was just loving God. I was giving God my all. I was singing from my heart. I wasn't ashamed to raise my hands and my voice in honor of my Father. I had no idea someone was watching. I was in a moment of true praise and worship. I may have even been crying. Not tears of sorrow but tears of joy for all of my blessings. I was getting my bucket filled up.

When you watch someone get renewed in their spirit, it's motivating. God is doing something special in their lives that we know nothing about. We don't know the circumstances of their walk or what kind of situation they may be in at the moment. In fact, we should be rejoicing with them that they had a breakthrough instead of judging them for being so emotional. When you get a good godly blessing, sometimes, your emotions just pour out of you. Sometimes, it's a release.

When you watch others in church, don't look at them and measure your own fellowship or closeness with God. Each of us is unique in our Christian walk. You get out of the praise-and-worship service what you put into it. You control you. As you worship, God meets you. Praise and worship opens up a floodgate to receive from God. You determine to what extent. If we all had the same needs, it would be different, but we don't. God looks on each of us individually.

Don't let anyone change your approach to God. When you worship and sing from your heart, God is the only thing that matters. Don't worry about who is watching. Don't look at your hands to see if they're in the right position as they're raised. No one cares how many rings you have or jewelry you're wearing. The show doesn't matter, but your heart truly does. You may be an example to others if they feel insecure about their own worship. Be you. Your fellowship with God is between you and Him. We're all different.

Let your praise and prayer come from your heart. Lip service means nothing. Extravagant words don't do anything for God. He wants your heart. Sing from your heart. Let it flow. Pray from your heart, and the words come easily. Your time with God is special. If others happen in on your love for God, they, too, may be blessed. Maybe they will get a glimpse of something they've never experienced before. Watching you may even make them bolder with their own Christian walk. Praise God and worship freely.

David danced before the Lord with all his might. He was ridiculed for doing so, but it didn't stop him. He had a special fellowship with God and was thankful for the blessing. Be like David. Dare to be different.

Challenge: Examine your relationship with God. Could you improve it? Worship in spirit and truth.

Give yourself margin to move, reflect, and respond. Even Jesus needed to be alone sometimes.

There's a difference between being alone and feeling alone. Feeling alone means you may feel abandoned and on your own in time of need. You may also feel rejection like you don't fit in. You have a need to be around others and depend on them for emotional support at times. It's human nature. Humans are social individuals. Feeling alone can be devastating. Rejection can be overwhelming. Just remember you have God.

On the flip side, sometimes, we need to separate ourselves to be alone. We purposefully establish boundaries and margins in order to reflect, regroup, and think. Processing emotions can take some downtime. Processing situations and refilling our emotional tank can take some alone time. Life can be overwhelming. Friends can be exhausting. Your ministry can be draining. You have to recharge yourself to be good again. You need to separate yourself to rest and reflect on you.

Giving people can quickly be drained. Our buckets are always being poured out. Unless we fill back up, we're not as effective as we should be. Taking time for yourself, alone, isn't a bad thing. Even Jesus chose to have some alone time. Several times throughout His ministry, He stepped away from the crowd and disengaged. In the Garden of Gethsemane, Jesus was alone and away from the disciples. He asked them to pray. They couldn't make it. He was alone with God. Traumatic events were about to happen, and He needed encouragement.

Other times, He just needed to rest. If you think about what He accomplished in three and half years, He had to be worn out. People were constantly around Him. He was followed everywhere He went. I'm sure His disciples were concerned that He never really turned anyone away and was constantly teaching. Then again, they were so enthralled by His ministry they themselves longed to be with Him all the time. Jesus was hardly ever alone. He had to take time for himself.

We, as Christians and believers, should model our lives after Jesus. There's nothing wrong with being alone to regroup. There's nothing wrong with telling someone you'll get back with them instead of making a split-second decision. There's nothing wrong with processing situations to reflect on the best and most logical solution. When others look up to you, they are ready and waiting for your words of wisdom. Your advice carries a lot of weight. You still have to pause and reflect.

If Jesus hadn't taken time for himself, He would have been emotionally and physically drained. That's not a good example of how to exist as a Christian. If we aren't refreshed and renewed, then our witness has lost its power. How we project ourselves makes a big difference to others. People are watching you. You need to set boundaries and margins to refresh yourself.

Ministering to others means your bucket is always being poured out. If you don't refill it, there's nothing more to give. You have to take time for yourself where you can get alone with God and refresh your physical, mental, and emotional self. Jesus modeled it for us. He even had to refill His bucket once in a while. Virtue was going out of Him. Performing miracles and teaching had to wear on Him. God blessed Him, but I'm sure He needed the space to heal himself.

Don't overextend yourself so that you're not positively affecting those around you. Find alone time to refresh, reflect, and process your days. You need to refill your bucket so that you can pour out to others. No one can recharge you except you. Take time to heal mentally, emotionally, physically, and spiritually.

Challenge: Set aside some time to be alone. Recharge yourself, and refill your bucket.

God directs your life. Doors open for opportunity. They also close for your protection and safety.

Many years ago, my life had taken a serious turn. Circumstances left me perplexed to the point that I didn't know what my future was going to be. I was so wrapped up in a "spiritual" life that I didn't know how to exist on my own. Honestly, I struggled with many things. I was dependent on others for my well-being and happiness. I didn't know anything but church. My pastoral family was first and foremost in my life, not God. Every two or three years, we would have to vote our pastor back into service or choose a new one. Every time this happened, I was an anxious mess. I didn't know how to exist without them.

It finally happened. They were leaving our church after about twelve years. My life was turned upside down. I had been so caught up in their lives that I didn't have one. They were my existence. I depended on them and loved them more than my own family at times. I was a mess. I was trying to hang onto them by a thin thread that was about to break. Everything in my life would change, even my home church. For two years, I never really felt grounded, so I attended different places looking for a fit.

This family finally settled back down in Cincinnati. In my determination to hold onto something that didn't exist, I applied for teaching jobs in and around that area hoping to relocate to be near them. After filing applications in twenty-five different school districts, I finally got an interview in Cincinnati public schools. I did well on the interview and was thinking that since it's a large school district, I should have a job. It didn't happen. No other calls for interviews out of twenty-five applications came. The door was closing, and I was trying my best to keep it pried open. God knew what He was doing.

That relationship was going downhill quickly. I was losing my footing and about to fall hard but didn't want to accept it. I was driving to Cincinnati every weekend to attend church. It was a three-hour one-way drive. When I think back, I should have listened to God, but my ears weren't tuned to Him. I wasn't hearing His voice.

I wasn't focused on Him. I was focused on survival and not being alone. Doors were closing.

I used to think to myself about applying for that many positions, being an experienced teacher, and not getting a job. I didn't understand why God was not answering my prayers. God was protecting me. I didn't see it then, but I did later. No matter how hard I tried to hang on, it wasn't meant to be. Eventually, I left everything for good and never looked back. I had taken my last three-hour drive. Door was closed. The thread was broken.

I was learning how to make it on my own. In order to do that, I needed God and my relationship with my family restored. God did answer my prayers. I was settling into my school life and devoting more time to what I needed to be focused on. I found a church and settled in. Most of all, I found God. God restored me. He restored my relationship with my family. It was difficult at first, but we managed to let things heal.

When I think back to how God saved me, I appreciate Him closing the door. The finality of it all came a few more years later. New doors were opening. More were closing too. I realized that God had a purpose for every chapter in my life. Yes, I survived. Just when I felt comfortable, God closed another door and I moved one thousand miles away. Again, God was protecting me and keeping me safe.

Starting a new life with new opportunities has been the best thing that ever happened to me. I am where God needs me to be right now. Doors will continue to open and close. I've learned not to push against them, though. It's all in His timing.

Challenge: Go through doors of opportunity with the same gusto you closed the doors behind you.

Prayer is the channel for which God pours blessings into our lives.

My mom wasn't always a Christian woman. She used to be quite the woman of words, so she tells it. I don't know when she actually became a believer, but I do know that she knew how to pray at a very young age. My mom had a dysfunctional upbringing. She was born in 1912, so when you think about life as she knew it then, it was a little challenging for anyone during those years. Her mother never married her father. My mom was mostly raised by her grandparents and uncles between Columbus, Ohio, and Fort Gay, West Virginia. She was well cared for and loved. My grandparents were godly people and taught her how to pray.

My mom told a story about the first prayer she ever prayed. She was five years old. As the story goes, she was walking home from school one afternoon and passed by a neighbor's house who had been baking. The aroma filled the air, and all she could think about was eating a piece of cake. She said she prayed to God that she would be invited into the house for cake. Her neighbor called her and invited my mom in, and her prayer was answered. She was ninety-one when she told me that story. She never forgot.

After my mom, Charlotte, became a believer, she was as tenacious and devoted a Christian as she was in the other sense. I'm thinking she could have held her own pretty well growing up too. She raised us all in church and made sure we were introduced to God at an early age. She was an amazing example of someone who prayed. I lived to hear it. Since I was number seventeen in my family, I experienced more of her praying for my older brothers and sisters. Her prayers saved our family and allowed God's blessings to cover us for generations.

The most awesome thing was having the privilege of listening to my mom pray in the wee hours of the morning. If I was up for water or going to the bathroom, I could hear her voice calling out to God on behalf of her children and grandchildren. She would name them one by one and ask God's blessings and safety for each. It was as if she knew God personally and was talking with Him. Gentle and kind. Those prayers have lingered in my mind over the years. I can still hear her praying in my thoughts. She's been gone twelve years.

I believe in the power of prayer. I believe that it is a direct channel to God from us. I believe He hears us and desires to have time with us. How else do we do it unless we pray? He's not asking for an elaborate prayer; simple is good. A prayer should be a conversation with God. He's not deaf, nor is He sleeping. He's waiting on us. If my mom hadn't demonstrated how to pray, I would have missed out on what I know in my own prayer life today. I talk with God. I enjoy talking with God. Does He answer? Yes. I listen.

If we are not bold enough to teach our children and grandchildren how to pray and connect with God, who will? God shouldn't be forced onto anyone, but being examples in our everyday lives sure goes a long way. My mom loved talking with God; otherwise, she wouldn't have spent so much time with Him. She knew that He heard her even in the wee hours of the night. She knew that God would bless her family for generations to come. Her prayers sustained us.

The next step is up to us to maintain that communication and be examples to our families as she was to us. Are we keeping that channel open so that God continues to bless us? After we're gone, will those in our families after us keep that channel open as well? Will we live on Mom's blessings, or have we established new ones? If our families don't know how to pray, will the link be broken? Will God continue to bless us? Don't be embarrassed to show your love for God in front of your children. Don't be afraid to call their names out to God. Chances are your child will be sitting in the hallway listening to you and learning. Keep praying.

Challenge: Keep an open channel of communication with God. Be a praying example to your family.

Evil is not always ugly and scary. Lucifer was beautiful and manipulating. Know the difference.

I enjoy watching documentaries and real-life crime stories. I'm fascinated by how the mind works. I'm more fascinated by how victims can be manipulated into thinking that evil is good. Children seem to be victimized the most. I attribute that to the ability of a child to trust almost any adult. It amazes me that a child can walk off with a complete stranger even though they've been told countless times not to do it. How many stories have we heard of children getting into vehicles with total strangers because they were manipulated into thinking that a total stranger would know anything about their family? It's mind blowing.

I enjoy real crime stories involving serial killers for some reason. I guess I love analyzing the facts and trying to figure out how a common individual can influence not one but many individuals into inescapable traps. What power do they hold? What characteristics do they possess that allow them to manipulate another individual into thinking they are a good person?

In most of the stories I've read or seen, serial killers have innate common characteristics besides being manipulative. Most are kind, gentle, and caring individuals who would do anything in the world for anyone in need. They are next-door neighbors whom you would trust to watch your kids or animals. They are everyday individuals who hold jobs in the community and encounter individuals all day long. They are the people you would see sitting beside you in church or at a school function. They are "good" people.

Evil people can have good intentions. Lucifer was God's angel of light. I'm sure it was a prominent position because he influenced others in his path of destruction. He allowed his position to make him feel so important and on the same level with God. Lucifer influenced one-third of the heavenly host of angels into believing that he was better than God. Can you imagine the side conversations going on as he talked with other angels and denied God? How could others be manipulated into following Lucifer after seeing God face-to-face and knowing the beauty of heaven? Lucifer looked good on the outside.

When God had finally had enough, Lucifer was kicked out of heaven. One-third of the angels believed his lies and followed him. Lucifer wasn't the ugly devil that he was portrayed to be. He was beautiful! God doesn't create evil and ugly; He creates beauty. Lucifer was so vain and caught up in himself that he actually thought he could overthrow God and gain heaven. Do you know someone with the same characteristics? People around us use good to do evil things. Even Christians can get caught up in evil by doing good.

Some of the most influential people are cult leaders. Think about their influence that may start with doing good and then turn evil when their egos can't handle the vainglory. Many even start out as Christians or godly believers. They start off teaching the Word of God but then twisting the scripture for their own self-pleasure. Victims endure the oppression because they can't see beyond the manipulation. The term used to describe it is *brainwashing*. Many have to be deprogrammed in order to get back to reality.

We are called to know those who labor among us. That means that if you are influenced by someone, make sure that the individual's beliefs truly line up with the Word of God. That means that *you* have to know the scripture. You can't take someone's word for truth. If their beliefs don't line up with God, then stop listening. Just because they are a "good" person doesn't mean they have good intentions. Study God's word. Know the scripture. Your knowledge helps you understand your surroundings. Don't be manipulated into believing something that's not godly based. Evil comes in different forms but mostly in disguises.

Challenge: Check your surroundings. Are those influencing you lining up with God?

Pray without stopping. Pray continuously. Don't wait for a good opportunity.

When you learn to pray, your words become easier. There's less fear in going before God. You are at ease in the presence of God. You respect God, but your thoughts and prayers flow easily when you continuously communicate with Him about things. It's easier to speak your heart instead of searching for just the right words to let Him know how you feel. As you learn to pray, sometimes, the Holy Spirit can take over and intercede for you. Usually, it's at a time when your heart is heavy, you are burdened down by life, or you are just overwhelmed to the point that you don't know what to say. Your comforter is there.

Jesus tells us to pray without stopping. Does that mean we go through our waking hours praying prayers to God? Actually, no, but wouldn't life be so much better if we were so wrapped up in God that it happened? "Praying without stopping," I believe, means to pray continuously. Here, again, do we do it all day long? I don't think so. I do believe, however, that continuous prayer helps us keep our mind focused.

One of the worst places to be is in the playground of our minds. The mind is a source for both good and bad. Have you ever been in the middle of doing something and a random evil thought crossed your mind? It just came out of nowhere. It's a fleeting moment but just enough to distract you. Sometimes, I just stop for a minute to try to figure out why and what. I shake my head and go on. Yes, there are times I have to ask God's forgiveness there on the spot. I believe our minds are a place of spiritual warfare.

When a fleeting thought passes through my mind, I can choose to dismiss it or entertain it. It can be as simple as craving a certain food or something as evil as revenge on a person. If I choose to dismiss the thoughts, I build up a resistance, and my prayers sustain me. I pray for God to take over and help me with what just happened. If I choose to entertain the thought, I am not trusting God and give in to temptation. So in this sense, I am continuously praying without stopping. I need to be prayer ready when my focus can change from good to bad in a split second. I need God to intervene on my behalf.

When my mind is focused on God, I have less time to worry and be distracted by daily things. When I give into worry, it consumes me whether I'm awake or asleep. My physical body feels it, and my emotions are a mess. I'm not effective when I'm distracted by what's going on in my mind. Learning to control my mind has been a challenge. Jesus must have known the same thing; otherwise, He wouldn't have stressed the importance of prayer. He was teaching His disciples that help comes from God and the Holy Spirit.

When I entertain negative thoughts, my well-being is compromised. I find myself being negative and complaining. I find myself being busy with situations that don't involve me. I don't project a very good Christlike image. I repent and ask God for help. We are told to put on the helmet of salvation for a reason. We need protection for our thoughts and feelings that stem from our minds. When we have a close personal relationship with God, our prayers flow more freely in time of need.

There's nothing wrong with being thankful in our prayers either. God does an amazing job of surrounding us with so many beautiful things. We don't always have to pray in times of need; we can pray prayers of thanks as well. We can pray prayers of thanks for the blessings we have received. Just enjoying life around us could keep us busy praying all day long.

Enjoy your time with God through the tough times as well as the wonderful blessings on us. Any time is good to pray. Don't wait for an opportune time; God doesn't wait for an opportune time to hear you.

Challenge: Increase your prayer time and communication with God. Be thankful for a change.

God has not given us a spirit of fear but a sound mind. It's up to us to maintain it.

In different situations growing up, I've heard the phrase "What goes in comes out." I think this can be applied to our physical body, our spiritual body, our emotional body, and our mental state. Of course, we are called to maintain our bodies because they are the temples of God. We need to have a spiritual balance in our lives in order to make sound decisions and represent well. I believe the most important, however, is maintaining our mental health.

All of these areas flow together, support one another, and help us maintain positive health. If anything in our lives is out of balance, we can become pretty miserable individuals. I know that when I snack too much on the wrong things, my system tells me I made a mistake. Spiritual balance is so vital. Knowing God's word and being able to have a true and honest relationship with God should be our focus. Our mental state is representative and affected by everything else.

Our family has been cursed by mental illness. I don't mean that we are bad people; many of us suffer from anxiety disorders and depression. I'm sure, genetically, you would find a common thread on both sides of my family tree. Probably the one who really struggled with the disease more was my mother. My dad never really showed much emotion. He was very low-key and passive. My mother, on the other hand, had bouts with anxiety that led to depression and sleeping a lot.

I always thought she was just worn out and tired from birthing seventeen children. You never know. Raising a large family was stressful, I'm sure. As a kid, I just remember her being so tired all of the time and sleeping a lot. For me, it was no fun, because I had to leave her alone instead of being around her. She was my mom. She didn't feel well all the time. It could have been that she was taking medications to help with the anxiety and depression, and it wasn't quite working. Back then, you didn't talk about mental illness.

She passed us the genes. I didn't recognize my illness until I was in my late thirties. Mine was triggered by stress. I was at the height of my career, burning candles at both ends, and not taking care of myself the way I should have been. I was drinking a pot of coffee a day and sometimes more just to keep up with everything. When I became sick, it hit me like a ton of bricks. I thought I was dying. I wanted to die sometimes. I couldn't handle being out of control. It all went back to my mental state.

In my case, anxiety and panic disorder stemmed from stress and caffeine. I remember being overwhelmed by the diagnosis. I didn't want to take medicine for the rest of my life, but I had a chemical imbalance that needed help. I cried and sobbed at the fact that I had limitations and my life changed. I had restrictions that only came from my mind. If I could control my mind, I could control the attacks.

When I moved a thousand miles away, my stress level decreased. I began focusing on God and myself. I exercised more and played softball. I had positive outlets. I could choose what I wanted to do instead of being guilted into doing what I didn't want to do. I felt free. My spiritual growth skyrocketed. I fell in love with God. My entire focus was on Him. My life was full of Him. When that happened, I began having balance in my life. Everything began coming together.

My mental health improved. I focused on the positive instead of the negative. I took in and fed positivity and love into my being. I was being healed. It took some distance to get there, but I made it. I'm still working on myself too. It's a battle sometimes, but I'm winning the war. God has taken control.

Challenge: Check to see if you need a tune-up. Are you balanced in your life? Focus on God, and fix it.

When you learn to trust, you learn to fly! Take the first step.

Is there something in your life that you haven't done that you wish you had? Have you ever been brave enough to take a leap of faith? Think about it. Everyone has a bucket list. What's holding you back from adventuring out beyond your comfort zone?

Several years ago, my colleague told me he wanted to go skydiving. That's a pretty daring thing to do. He asked if I wanted to go. I was reluctant at first but took him up on the offer. I had never really thought about doing it, but the more I thought about it, I thought, *Why not? What could possibly go wrong?* He made the appointment, and we headed out to the airport.

Upon arrival, my nerves were even having anxiety. What was I thinking? I've seen pictures and videos of people skydiving but never pictured myself doing it. We paid the fee, and they led us into a little side room to explain the rules. We signed the waivers and agreed that they would not be responsible for our injuries. We decided to tandem jump.

They suited us up and explained the process. Basically, an actual professional skydiver would be attached to my back. He would be the one to pull the chute and guide us safely as we soared across the sky. Oh, and by the way, did I want pictures and a video? Of course! If I was risking my life for this once in a lifetime experience, I was getting it all! I suited up and headed toward the plane. It looked small. It was.

We ascended up to ten thousand feet. Our pilot radioed us to say that we had reached our altitude to jump. The diver strapped himself on my back very tightly and kept telling me not to worry. We inched closer to the open door ten thousand feet up in the air. Looking straight out of the plane, all I saw was blue sky. My nerves kicked in. I wanted to say no; but before I could respond, I was at the edge of the exit, ready to fly.

I was propelled forward before I could even think about backing out. We were falling into thin air. Free falling is very scary! I don't remember a lot of what happened initially, because I think I lost consciousness for a few seconds. The parachute opened, and I became alert enough to look around to see that I was soaring! I was floating through the air. The ground looked so far away, and I could see for miles! It was absolutely breathtaking. At one point, I was allowed to guide the parachute, and then my diver took over. We landed safely on the ground.

I trusted a stranger to keep me safe. I didn't even know this guy. I knew his credentials. He reassured me every step of the way. He let me guide the chute. He instructed me how to land. He let me enjoy the scenery as we floated through the sky. I didn't have a choice to disobey him, because he was strapped to my back. Where he went, I went.

This is similar to our relationship with God. We entrust Him to guide us and keep us safe. When we don't know exactly what we're doing, He's there to take over and reassure us that everything is going to be okay. He allows us to enjoy the beauty of life as He guides us through our circumstances. He truly has our back. Where He goes, we go if we are truly trusting Him. It's our choice. Without complete trust, it's hard to take a leap of faith. He's got us in His hands. Through the good and the bad, God is always there for us.

Think about what we would miss out on or the blessings in our lives if we chose to say no. Trusting God should be easy. Our fears are our apprehensions. When you trust God, you soar.

Challenge: Put your trust in God, even when your circumstances seem insurmountable. He's got your back.

Faithfulness is more than just showing up to church every Sunday and calling yourself a Christian. Be a faithful servant.

To be faithful can be described as someone who is loyal, steadfast, reliable, and consistent. Those who keep their promises are faithful. Think of a person who is faithful to you. What characteristics stand out about that person? I have many people in my immediate circle who are faithful. I know that if I need something, they would be the first to come to my aid. They would take care of me, have my back, and stand by my side no matter what. Are you faithful? Do you fit the same characteristics?

If those around you were asked to describe you, would one of those words be *faithful?* Are you loyal, dependable, honest, or consistent? Take a step back, and reevaluate who you are. Maybe you're faithful and reliable to some but not others. God calls us to be good and faithful servants.

When you show up for church every Sunday, does that make you a faithful servant? Just because you're taking up space and breathing air, are you faithful? Well, let's look at this situation. Showing up every Sunday, volunteering your time in the ministries of the church, and going through the motions mean you're dependable and consistent. Some people are even steadfast because they really don't enjoy giving up their spot on a pew. They can even get downright defensive. That's consistent, but is it a faithful servant?

Growing up in church, I was consistent, dependable, reliable, steadfast, and loyal; but I wasn't always a faithful servant. I called myself a Christian, but am ashamed to say that I wasn't sometimes. Just because I was involved in the different ministries of the church didn't make me a Christian. To serve others is a high calling. When Jesus called the twelve disciples, He called them servants. He taught them to serve others according to the will of God. This was a new twist on Christianity.

Being a servant means that you're attending to others. You humble yourself before others to understand a greater level of giving as Jesus did. There is no reward or recognition. You are learning lessons by sacrificing your ego and personal insecurities. You are putting yourself in a position of submission so that others recognize your willingness to give of yourself. Your submission isn't to people but to the will of God. The act of serving as a Christian is to glorify God. A true servant's heart is honored by God.

Can you serve in a church and volunteer your time and still not be a faithful servant? Yes, you can. If your heart is not in tune with the will of God, I believe that you are only doing a faithful duty. Does going to church every Sunday mean that you are a Christian? No, it doesn't. There's one way to the cross, and except you go through Jesus, you're not a true believer. It means you are a reliable person. You need to be saved through the blood of Jesus and remission of your sins. Simply, ask God to forgive you of your sins, and believe He does. He will.

Many times, when I was working in the different ministries of the church, I was simply going through the motions of my duties. I was a burned-out servant. My heart was not in it. At some points, I dreaded being at church. I disliked spending my entire weekend at or in church services. I became negative and kept complaining. I was a mess. I still had God in my heart. That saved me.

A faithful servant chooses to follow the will of God and be an extension of grace, mercy, and love. Jesus was the greatest example for us to follow. God recognizes good and faithful servants. Join the group.

Challenge: Be a faithful servant to others. Your characteristics show your willingness to humbly serve.

When you prioritize your life, put needs before wants. Needing God is more than wanting God.

According to the Bible, we have the option of choosing God. Yes, He created us in His image. Yes, He will never leave us or forsake us. Yes, He will fight our battles for us. Yes, He will calm our storms and wipe away our tears. He will take our fears and turn mourning into laughter. Yes, He will give us the desires of our hearts. But if we don't choose Him, will He?

There is a distinct difference between "needing" God and "wanting" God. When we have the need for a car, we get the most reliable and fuel efficient for our needs. When we want a car, we pay way too much for the added features and the extra packages. Do we need them? Probably not. The car salesman makes the car look so amazing that we overspend and blow our budget. We could have a more reliable fuel-efficient car that may not look too good on the outside but serves its purpose. The expectation is different.

With God, when we need Him, we are usually in a situation where all hope seems lost. We are willing to sacrifice everything we have and vow to stay loyal if He just gets us out of trouble. How many times have you called out to God in the midst of your pain and suffering, expecting God to rush in and save you just in the nick of time? You are choosing to "need" God at your convenience. Once your troubling situation has passed, where do you prioritize God? Is He placed on the back burner until next time? Yes, He usually is.

When you "want" God, you are willing to sacrifice everything you have for a relationship with Him. It's not a one-time deal or just when you "need" Him. You desire to praise and worship Him and bless Him regardless of His blessings on you. You choose to love Him because He loves you. You desire to communicate with Him because He cares for you. You don't have to ask for favor; you're already given favor. You are given what you need. God loads you daily with blessings. He doesn't require much from you except a relationship. He is your rock, stability, anchor, healer, redeemer, waymaker, miracle worker, promise keeper, and light in the darkness. That's truly who

He is. You don't have to beg for His attention, He's already there. He knows everything about you.

Let's go back to the car. I remember my first car was a hand-me-down Dodge Aspen. It was already pretty used when I inherited it. I put the basic liability insurance on it, and off I went. I didn't make it too far, however, because it had a hole in the gas tank. I kept putting gas in; it kept leaking out. It was probably a fire hazard to begin with, but I needed wheels to get me around. I drove it until it died. Keep in mind that my radius of driving was very limited. I knew how far I could go before I had to put enough gas in to make it where I needed to be. It was challenging. Does this sound like your relationship with God?

Have you limited yourself to a restricted area of growth and trust because you "need" God? Are you constantly running out of gas because you have a leak in your tank? Are you praying to God because you want to or because you need His favor to make it to the next stop? Are you hoping God will bail you out and keep you safe as you travel even short distances? If you answer yes, then you need God, not want God.

A wanted relationship with God is long-term. There is mutual respect and trust. You can live each day knowing that He will be there no matter what happens. He knows your steps and prepares your way. You want to talk with Him. You embrace worship and praise Him. You are not limited on your path. You have protection and grace beyond belief. You want to spend time with Him. You "want" God.

Challenge: Choose to want God over needing God. When you prioritize your life, keep Him first.

Sometimes, you have to make difficult decisions. Let God guide you in the right direction, not people.

Many times in my life, I was under the impression that I was doing what was right. Afterward, I realized I had hurt others and caused distances that I felt would be unable to bridge. Most of the issues in my early adulthood stemmed from church or family. I had diluted my personal life and needs into dependency upon others who I thought were leading me in the right direction. I was so absorbed by church activities and volunteering that I neglected what was really important to me…my family.

From the outside, my family and friends saw my dilemma. They tried to talk with me and bring me back around. It didn't work. I was doing what I thought I should be doing. I spent every waking hour trying to please and get the approval of those who simply used me. I was vulnerable and was taken advantage of very discreetly. It was sucking the life out of me. I was exhausted most of the time from working a full-time teaching job to doing total church activities on the weekends. I didn't see it. I was made to believe that my sacrifices and work would earn me better credibility with God.

Getting together with my family was very awkward. I felt very out of place and really didn't have much to talk about, because I had lost touch with who my family was. I even attended the same church as some of my family, and we didn't speak. I thought I was in the right for some reason. I was devoting my time and full attention to matters that just made my life difficult. Yet I was still being used. I didn't see it then.

I was accepted at family gatherings, but my devotion and atten- tion were elsewhere. I was seeking approval from those who I now know really didn't care about me. I was struggling with mental health issues like depression and anxiety but hadn't yet been diagnosed or receiving help. When I tried to understand things, I accepted every bad situation as my fault, and I had to ask forgiveness from God. I couldn't have feelings about issues because I would be rejected. My family still accepted me and put up with my foolishness to fit into a bad situation.

After I left my home church, I had trouble settling in anywhere. There just wasn't a connection. After a few years of trying to hold on to a broken relationship of use and distrust, I tried even harder to please. I drove almost four hours every weekend to serve in a church where I thought things would be different. It wasn't. I got pushed farther and farther away. I sacrificed my downtime over each weekend and was still unappreciated. I was wearing down fast from the mental and physical exhaustion. I made conscious decisions, but they weren't the right ones. I would drive for four hours to get home on Sunday nights while crying the entire way. I knew what I was doing wasn't right, but I didn't know how to fix it. This lasted for months.

I had a decision to make. Since I was disappearing into oblivion, it was a good time to take a break. I had to consciously begin taking care of myself. No one could make the decision for me. God knew I had to experience some things to be able to see the whole situation. I was trying to make things happen, and He was trying to lead me out. I made the last, long Sunday night drive home while crying all the way. I was done.

The separation and uncaring attitude of those who I thought cared about me helped me realize what I'd been told all along. I had sacrificed my family for nothing. Broken relationships had to be mended. Trust had to be built all over again. I had really made a mess of things. I knew I had a tough road ahead of me too. I also knew that now that I was on the right track, God was leading the way. I decided to follow this time. Eventually, yes, my love and respect for my family replaced the loss of a dream. I was healing.

Challenge: Think about how decisions affect you and those closest to you. False hope can lead you down a long, tough road. You'll learn lessons, but you'll also be wearing a lot of scars.

God doesn't identify you by your religion when He hears your cry or sees your tears. He loves you.

It's very easy to get caught up in religion and lose sight of God. It happens to all people from all walks of life. It happens to Christians, non-Christians, pastors, bishops, and religious leaders. If you think about it, God didn't come up with religion. Man did. Man took the Word of God, interpreted it for what was chosen, added a few other stipulations that were "backed" by the Bible, and added a title to their newfound belief. Think about all of the names of churches and religions in the world today.

When God created the world, it was pretty simple. There was God, and God's word. There was a free relationship with the early prophets where actual conversations occurred between God and man. There were times when God had to be reminded of His promises when He was so upset that He was going to annihilate an entire group of people. He had reasons, of course, but had to be reminded of His covenant more than once. That's a pretty close relationship with God.

So I'm wondering what He was thinking when, all of a sudden, He hears Christianity popping up in different sects in different parts of the world. I can see Him shaking His head and wondering what happened after He made it so easy for everyone. A few simple commands should have gone a long way. How hard it must be for Him to ignore what man has created in different religions.

The good thing is, He's still sticking by His words. When we approach Him, He doesn't look at us as a Baptist, Pentecostal, Methodist, or even Episcopalian. He looks at us as a human. He understands who He created and what the purpose is for each and every one of us. He understands our hearts and sees our tears. He understands our pain, disappointment, and hurts. He just wants to love us. Thankfully, doctrine doesn't get in the way.

When I go to God, I approach with a sincere heart and desire to talk with Him. There are times I cry out to Him because of situations. There are times I go before Him and have no words at all. I listen. Many times, I've gone to Him for healing or on behalf of a friend. God knows my heart. He doesn't have to look up what religion I identify with to see if He's making the right move for me. He's not worried about offending me if He doesn't align with what I believe. He's God. He loves me.

I'm thankful that I don't have to wait for a certain time or place to approach God. I can pray anywhere I feel the need or desire. I don't have to be on my knees to reach God. I can be driving, walking, in the gym, at school, or even in a crowd to get His attention. Believe it or not, I can call on God when I'm not sitting in a church. Jesus made a way for all of us to approach God freely. God tore the veil into pieces so that anyone can approach God in heaven. There's no ritual performed or special sacrifice to get His attention. He's right there for each of us.

When you approach God, He's there. When you cry out to Him, He hears you immediately. When you need help, He's available. Jesus bridged the gap between man and God. He was the ultimate sacrifice so that it would be easier for us to communicate with God. It was unbelievable to most people who heard Jesus teach and preach in person. It was a new concept they never heard of. They believed, and so should we.

God is as close as a brother, sister, or family member. You don't have to dial Him up; He's always available. He never sleeps or slumbers. He accepts you for you and not your religious beliefs.

Challenge: Don't let religion stand in your way of approaching God. He doesn't recognize it.

It doesn't matter what color you paint a lie; it's still a lie. Being truthful holds so much more credibility.

I was born with the innate ability to be truthful. I can't help it. I was taught not to tell a lie, and I knew if I did and got caught, I was in huge trouble. So I perfected the ability to stretch the truth. If you don't know what that means, here's a simple explanation. I speed all the time. If I get caught, I probably should not fight the ticket, because I know I speed.

Getting pulled over means the first question I usually get asked is, "Do you know how fast you were going?" Well, I usually have a pretty good idea but not the exact number, but I respond with, "I'm not really sure." And then I proceed to tell the officer that this is the first time I've ever driven in this area and I was admiring all the beautiful hills and countryside. I wasn't really paying attention. He takes my information and goes to his car. Upon returning, I ask if he can tell me where a certain place is that I'm supposed to be meeting someone. He helps me out, gives me a warning, and sends me on my way.

So, technically, I didn't lie, but I may have stretched the truth a little bit. That one really did happen. And, yes, I was not paying attention. Sometimes, I can't work myself out of something, and I get nailed with a hefty fine. I deserve it. This is a little different, however, from actually telling false information about someone, which usually leads to trouble. Growing up in church, we had people who were known as "talebearers." Another nice word is someone who spreads gossip about others. Most of the time, it's not truthful information.

Even though there are different words to describe someone who tells false information about others, they are basically still liars. If they intentionally say something false about someone, they are telling false information that could hurt someone's credibility. I would not expect Christians or godly people to be the ones to spread rumors, but it does happen. If you're in the know, you feel a need to tell others. Many times, confidential information has been breached which then robs someone of their self-worth. Sometimes, individuals never recover.

If we, as humans, could manage to keep our attention on God, then we might be less worried about what is happening with those around us. We might be less likely to join in on conversations about other individuals who are on the receiving end of false information being shared about them. The more we step back and evaluate the situation, the more likely no one will get hurt.

I've been involved in situations where false information was told about me. My first thought was to react with slander toward the individual who lied. My next reaction was to go to them, face them, tell them how I feel about them, and then physically hurt them for ruining my day. But I didn't do that. That's one of those "what would Jesus do" moments. I realized that the truth always comes out and rises to the surface. I just ride the wave till it happens. Then the liar is the one who looks foolish for spreading false information.

I think Christians can be very critical of others. Maybe that's why they look for someone to sin so they can treat them as less of an individual than they are. Bearing false news about someone makes them look like they're important maybe. Truth is, no one wants to be around those individuals. You learn to steer clear of them at all costs. Liars can use their voice for good. The problem is that they've perfected the art of tearing someone else down. Sometimes, it seems to come naturally to them. In the end, however, their reputation is a tarnished one.

Challenge: Use your words to encourage and lift others up instead of tearing them down. If you have nothing good to say, don't say it. Let your every word glorify God.

Enticing situations can suck you in and leave you miserable. They can ruin your life.

Back in the forties, fifties, and sixties, a lot of what we saw in the few media outlets we had were very censored when it came to sexual immorality and violence. I remember growing up in the late sixties when we had three major television channels and a VHS box to get reception. If we couldn't see the picture clearly, someone had to turn the outside antenna to get good reception. By then, the limited program was over.

Much of what we saw was very family oriented and safe for all ages. Even the catalogs that were mailed out barely showed any skin. Swimsuits were one piece, and you rarely saw any ads for underwear. Things were so very private. That's the way the world was. The family morals and social expectations were very godly oriented. It seemed like you were an outcast if you didn't go to church.

As our society changed, so did the media outlets. Censorship eased up when it came to what was being shown on television and in the movies. The late sixties brought around the sexual revolution. It was everywhere. Our eyes were opened to so much more provocative material and content. Privacy didn't mean anything anymore. We were exposed to so much more and from all sides. The sacred marriage bond was challenged in so many different ways.

As the computer age ramped up, so did our access to more immoral material that threatened family bonds and existence. Even children had access to inappropriate material and violence. It was so easily accessible. It seemed like immorality had walked right into our houses and taken up residency.

The existence of adultery has been around for ages. The solid marriage vow that once prevailed has been challenged. Adulterous affairs are reported at the highest political positions and at the highest Christian level. We are all human. That still doesn't give us the right to have intimate relationships with others outside of marriage. That's adultery. That's what God warned about. He said not to do it.

Our society leans more toward the idea that it's okay to have relationships outside of marriage. Even Moses gave the okay to children of Israel for divorce. Hanging out in the desert probably became pretty enticing to look elsewhere for love, strength, and encouragement. That's usually what happens. We find someone who is willing to make us feel better, even though we've gone against God's word. Inside is the moral dilemma of knowing that it's not pleasing to God but fulfills a human desire. It's like an addiction.

I believe that adultery hurts not only a marriage but also the family unit. Unless marriages are mended and relationships are rebuilt, the entire family suffers. How many times have adulterous affairs ended up in divorce where the children are caught between parents and bad custody situations? It's not their fault. The adults allowed themselves to wander away from what they know is true and right, and they then got sucked into a miserable situation.

Let's go back to the situation where you first considered being with someone other than your spouse. What made you look away? What was worth forfeiting your marriage with the person you loved till death was going to part you? You could have walked away. You could have said no. The answer is simply that you're human, and sometimes, it's easier to mess up than fight for what you know is right. Be the godly man or woman to preserve your family. Don't fall for the tricks of the enemy and be enticed into a bad situation.

Challenge: Reevaluate your marriage and family. Reevaluate your relationship with God. Is He in the center of it all?

God gave us a day of rest from our labor. It helps us prepare for the next six days coming up.

When the children of Israel came out of Egypt, some of them had forgotten the feasts, events, and celebrations that had been set aside to honor God. In the time of Abraham, Isaac, and Jacob, God was honored and admired by the people. When they lived in Egypt, they probably forgot about God and their heritage. God had a covenant with Abraham that the Israelites would multiply like the sands of the sea. God's covenant was still in place in Egypt, even though Abraham was long gone.

Remember the Sabbath, and keep it holy. The Sabbath is day seven. Some people observe the seventh day on Saturday. Most observe it on Sunday. Many calendars have existed over the years, and it really doesn't matter much. Today's calendar uses the weekdays as Monday through Friday. Saturday is the sixth day, and Sunday the seventh. So however it is observed doesn't really matter.

Because the children of Israel had to be retaught the covenant of God, observance of the seventh day was needed. God even used six days to create the world and rested on the seventh. In likeness, we are busy with our lives six days out of the week and need to take time to observe God and be thankful for our blessings at least one day out of the week.

Growing up, Sundays were set aside for church service. We went to Sunday school, morning worship, and evening service all in one day. It was exhausting sometimes. As a kid, Saturday was the day to have fun, and maybe I could squeeze in a few hours on Sunday before evening service. This only meant that all homework had to be done on Saturday or Friday because I was so tired after church services all day on Sunday that I just wanted to go to bed. No, we weren't allowed to miss church. Yes, Sunday was observed.

As an adult, I learned to appreciate the value of Sunday and giving my time to God. I believe that me sitting in a seat at my church allows me to get away from the world. I have time set aside for God. I have to focus on Him. I don't have my cell phone to distract me like others I see in church. I still carry my Bible and don't need to have an app on my phone. I am truly zoned into God.

Our lives are so taken away with distractions. Technology has overloaded us with information. We are at the point in our lives that we could literally sit at home and not leave our houses for days, weeks, or even months at a time. We can now watch church online. It can be a convenience if you can't get out, though. The Word of God is reaching around the globe.

When I am sitting at church, my full attention is on God. Everything I do is about God. I still might get a little distracted but not as if I was home. My life is so demanding through the week that I just forget how to take time for myself and realize how blessed I really am. Saturday is for rest. Sunday is for God. That's how I see it. I pour my life into my career and into helping others that I need the weekend to refuel and recharge for the next week. Being fed the Word in church is my refueling station.

Sunday is a day to honor God. He blesses us with so much that we would be dishonoring Him if we didn't recognize Him throughout the day. Our recognition doesn't have to be all day. He doesn't require that from us. I'm sure He realizes we have busy lives. He understands that we need time for ourselves too. If we can't be good to ourselves, we can't be good to others. God knew that in the beginning.

Let every day be a day to honor and thank God. Don't wait until the Sabbath.

Challenge: Be in church away from distractions. Give God your true attention. Spend some alone time with Him. He blesses you through the week; honor Him through the day.

God commands us to not have any other god before Him.

I remember spending a good portion of my young adult life seeking attention and approval of my close friends. I was so busy trying to please them that my eyes were slightly diverted from God. At the time, their approval and attention meant more to me than even my own family. I didn't really see the ramifications of a truly bad situation until I pulled myself out of it.

My misunderstanding and hurt were that of how could my friends dote over and have time for others when they never had time for me? I was used to the point of physical exhaustion. I spent my money to make sure that they had what they needed. I felt obligated to take care of them, yet I was jealous. They never had quality time for me. It was hard for me to grasp the concept after giving so much of myself to them.

The children of Israel had been taken care of in Egypt. After Joseph had passed away and the new pharaoh saw how mighty in number they were, he decided to make them slaves. Maybe God's intention was for them to stay in Egypt a little longer. The only problem was that the first generation that moved to Egypt was also gone. The following generations didn't really have a connection with God. Somehow, they had lost the honor and glory for God. I'm sure they also began idol worship from hanging with the Egyptians.

God saw what was unfolding and had to move them out of Egypt. It took some doing, but it was accomplished. In the wilderness, they longed for bondage and material things. Their focus wasn't on God. God provided everything for them, and still they complained. How could you want to be in bondage rather than be rewarded and taken care of? Moses met with God on Mt. Sinai, and the Ten Commandments were given to guide the people.

The very first one was not to have any other god before God. The idol worship had to go. God was a jealous God. He had provided for them, brought them out of bondage, and held their future and prosperity in His hands; and yet they couldn't keep Him first in their lives. He longed for undivided attention and worship. He longed to communicate with them and love them. I'm sure He had moments where He wanted to annihilate them. He had done everything for them, yet they turned their back on Him and chose another.

Even as Moses was talking with God up on the mountain, Aaron had built a golden calf for them to worship. He was afraid they were going to go berserk on him. These people were used to tangible gods that they had with them all the time. Moses descended from the mountain, ground up the idol into powder, poured it into the water, and made the people drink the water. That had to taste pretty badly. Maybe they needed to be filled up with their idols before they realized who God really was.

God looks on us with a jealous spirit. How many times has He delivered us from tragedy, heartache, sickness, and pain to be put on the back burner by our activities and material things we idolize? A god is considered a supernatural being and revered as divine. A god can also be anything that takes the place of God, our righteous deity. Think about this. Anything that stands between you and God is closer to God than you are. So when your family, job, money, business, or even hobbies take up so much of your time that you neglect God, that could be your god.

God had to take the children of Israel through a desert forty years before their focus turned back to Him. Many generations died without seeing the Promised Land. We need to get back to where our only focus is on God. The first commandment was the turning point. It was time to regroup. And they did.

Challenge: Focus on God. Get rid of the other things in your life that have replaced Him. He misses you.

Your life is so filled with blessings and loving people God has placed in your life over the years. Be thankful. He meant to do it.

Have you ever thought about someone and felt impressed to call them or check on them? It happens to me all the time. Luckily, we don't have to memorize phone numbers anymore. That is one technology invention that I truly enjoy. I pick up the phone and call or sometimes text. The funny thing is that there are people whom I call and talk with and I haven't spoken with in years. Our conversation doesn't reflect that, though. We talk for long minutes just like we had spoken last week.

God will lay someone on my heart. I usually pray for them first and then try to reach out to them. Sometimes, I learn that they had been going through a rough patch and needed a little prayer to pick them up. I am very good about acting on what God gives me. I don't feel badly about calling; I just do. I don't feel bad that I haven't talked with them for a while. Life happens, and time gets taken up by other things.

I have to say that I have been so very blessed to have met so many amazingly loving people in my lifetime. I am very good about keeping in contact with old friends. Just because I move away or get busy with life, there is usually a time when I need to reconnect. Social media has made it very easy to keep in contact even though I haven't seen people for a long period of time.

The one good thing is that people also try to reconnect with me. I started teaching in 1985. I started working at an elementary school, so many of my kids were in third and fourth grades. Believe it or not, some of those students found me on social media and still keep in contact. It makes me feel good that I made an impact on them so that they want to reconnect with me. Many of my students from those early years are now married with kids and grandkids. It's crazy to think that I knew them before they even began to think about having a family.

Since I am still teaching, I get those kind notes from my former students that let me know how much they appreciated me and what a good job I did. They want to let me know how well they have succeeded. I love hearing about their lives and watching them grow still into adulthood. Some of my kids will be my kids forever. God placed them into my life for a reason. They became a part of my family when they met me in class.

I still have the opportunity to keep in touch with so many of my amazing coworkers from different schools too. Even though some of us have moved a great distance away, we still have that family tie from growing up together and teaching together for years. There's a special common bond that can't be broken. I have been blessed so many times by kids recognizing me in public and actually stopping to say hello. It's a feeling that just can't be explained. Sometimes, I feel like a celebrity.

It makes me feel so good that I had an impact on someone else's life. I always say that if I didn't do a good job, they wouldn't want to talk with me. Be thankful for those whom God has placed in your life. Even those who are your family have been handpicked by God. He places us together for a reason. He allows us to bond for a purpose. You never know when you may get a phone call from someone in your past who has been thinking about and praying for you. It's a good feeling to know that they are still there for you.

Don't miss out on the impact you can make on someone's life. At some point, they may really need your love and guidance again. Just be available and pretend you talked with them yesterday.

Challenge: Your life is filled with amazing people. Stop and take notice of who they are. Love them.

Being a Christian doesn't mean you don't rely on those put into your path to help you. Yes, God can perform miracles, but He also uses people so they can be a blessing and help to others.

A child's faith is amazingly strong. Even Jesus said to come to God with the faith of a child. Children are so very trusting of others. That's also why they are often taken advantage of as well. Their whole lives are centered around needs being fulfilled. When they ask, it's usually given. That's the faith adults need to have.

When I was a kid, I was taught that if I was sick, God could heal me. I was prayed over for toothaches, headaches, body aches, flu, and any other illness that I contracted. When I asked for prayer, my pastor would break out the oil, anoint me, and pray; and it's done. I walked away believing that I was going to be healed instantly. Did it happen instantly? No, it didn't. Did I feel better? Yes, I did. Maybe it was my faith. Maybe it really was a miracle. I knew that in any situation, God had my back and would take care of me. I just asked.

Even as a child, I knew that if I had a need to go to a doctor, I was trusting that the doctor would give me the right medicine and take care of me. I believed that God had given the doctor the knowledge to be able to diagnose what was wrong and help me feel better.

As an adult, I still believe that God can heal me. I struggle with mental health issues because of my diagnosis of anxiety and panic disorder but also depression. Before I even reached out to a doctor, I had tried to trust God to help me. I struggled a lot. I was fighting an uphill battle all the time. I was existing in life but not being very productive. It was like I was held captive by something that I couldn't control. It was nonstop.

When I finally reached out to mental health professionals thinking that there was a quick fix, I found out that I would have to be on medication, probably long-term. I bawled. I didn't want to be dependent on medicine to feel good. I was physically healthy, so why couldn't my brain function properly? It was one of the worst periods of my life that I endured. I finally found the doctor who helped me understand and balance my medication. I learned to deal with my condition. I loved my doctor for finally helping me find some relief.

During my ordeal, I was sitting in a church service where the minister spoke about faith in God and trusting God for everything. He stated that if you're sick, go to God. You don't need to go to a doctor to find peace. God can take care of it. God can heal any ailment. God can fix any situation. And even though I do believe that, I was dumbfounded and embarrassed that I had to see a mental health doctor and was taking medicine. I felt ashamed like I wasn't trusting God. I knew I was doing the right thing.

I didn't agree with what was being said and thought back to how many times this same minister had seen doctors for ailments because of needing expertise and help. I realized that pastors and ministers are human. They're not doctors. They're not mental health professionals. Sometimes, they can give bad advice, and people trust them to do and say the right thing. How many times have I seen them tell people to throw out their medicine and trust God? How many times have people come to them saying they want to stop taking medicine and trust God and they said it was okay?

God gives knowledge to individuals with expertise to be able to help us and bless us. If we didn't have professionals in certain areas, we might be suffering more than we are. God doesn't expect us to harm ourselves for the sake of someone else. God puts people in our paths to help us be better in all areas of our lives. I trust pastors for my spiritual journey. When it comes to my physical or mental health, I find a professional. I believe God can heal me, but in the meantime, I can use what He's already given me.

Challenge: Let God bless you through others. Have faith, but also be smart about who you listen to.

Some people choose a life of solitude without much human interaction. Some live their lives without human interaction but not by choice.

Mother Teresa was notorious for loving those who were unlovable. Her entire life was spent taking care of those who had been lost in the world, considered untouchable, and left alone to die. I can imagine that there were so many people who saw her kind face and compassionate eyes as they left this earth. She was the only family they had. She never gave up on them, and she fought for them to the end.

Think about how many individuals you pass by in a day through your daily routine, who need someone to love and appreciate them. They, too, have routines in their day; but sometimes, it doesn't involve communication or acknowledgment of any kind. They simply slip into the cracks without anyone noticing that they even exist. Look deeply; you may even see it in their eyes. After a while, it's obvious.

When I was teaching high school, I took the position as the senior class advisor. I enjoyed getting to know the kids and helping them have fun planning all of the events for their last year of school. There were so many things to do. I taught in a rural school where many families were related or the kids had grown up in the same neighborhoods for most of their lives. They knew each other like family.

I will never forget standing at duty by the back door one day when a tall kid came through to go to buses. I told him to have a great evening and called him by name. He stopped and looked straight at me. He told me that I was the first teacher at my school to ever recognize him and call him by his name. I was taken aback a bit. He wasn't one of my students, but I had recognized his name from compiling list of names for graduation. He went on out the door and to his bus.

Those few seconds changed my life. I'm sure he probably thought about it as well. How many times in life do we get looked over or passed by? It's not that we need recognition, but hearing our name being called surely makes a difference. I know that in a conversation if someone says my name, it makes me pay attention more to what's being said. My attention is needed and wanted. I have value. I matter.

When God forms us, He knows us by name. With billions of names to know and remember, God remembers mine. When He calls my name, I perk up and pay attention. I stop for a second and realize that God knows me by name. He needs my attention. I have value. I matter. The same goes when I pray and talk with Him. He knows my voice. He listens. He loves hearing from me.

Yes, there are those who choose to live alone and are very happy. They don't require much affirmation and human interaction. There are also those who could use a smile or a kind word. Simple recognition doesn't have to be much. A nod or kind gesture can start a ripple effect in someone's life. Just acknowledging that someone exists can be a life changer.

When we reach out to those in need, it doesn't have to be something that takes a huge toll on our own lives. We need to learn to see others, though, and love them for who they are. We don't know the circumstances that surround them at the moment. We just need to be kind. We don't live in their shoes.

God places individuals in our path every day. They are there for a reason. Maybe they help save our lives too. Love those who need it. Help those who are less fortunate. Recognize those in need.

Challenge: See those around you. Be kind to everyone. That way you won't miss an opportunity.

The path you have chosen is yours. It's your means to the end goal. It doesn't matter how long it takes you to get there; just get there.

In my class, we talk a lot about career choices and what my kids want to be when they graduate from high school. It overwhelms them sometimes because they aren't thinking that far ahead. I can see their anxiety level rising right before me. I remind them that it's a goal. We talk about how you have to want to do something and high school helps prepare you for what you want to do when you graduate. Unless, of course, you want to live with your parents the rest of your life. Some don't see that as a bad choice.

We talk about my career choice and why I wanted to be a teacher. I tell them that ever since I was a little kid, I wanted to be a teacher. The reality is I wanted to be a missionary. I so admired the strong biblical figures who were missionaries and got to tell others about God for the first time. I heard stories of the martyrs and how they gave their lives for God and His work. I read about and listened to present-day missionaries who simply gave of themselves to share Jesus with others who had never heard of Him. That was my choice. I had no doubt that I could do it. In high school, I chose teaching as my career.

Throughout high school, I prepared for teaching by taking the college prep classes that would help me in the next step of my life. I was going to teach. I started out with a desire to teach early childhood and then changed my mind. Elementary suited me better. I took my classes, prepared myself, and graduated with a degree. I made it! I was a teacher! My career began.

I was hired as a long-term substitute for a special needs tutor to finish out the year. I took an elementary position. I knew I had to get my foot in the door any way possible and begin building my resume. I knew I could handle these kids. I was assigned to grades kindergarten through grade five. Never underestimate the power of an elementary student during the cold and flu season. They can take out any adult with one sneeze. Yes, they were germy.

On the very first day of my new job, a little third grader showed up. Our conversation went something like this. I asked him if he had any work that he needed to do. He told me he had a report to write. I said, "Good. What are you going to write it on?" He said, "Paper, duh." I knew then I had found my spot in life.

I lasted at that elementary school several years and then went on to a high school for fourteen years. All the while, I was working with kids with special needs. These kids turned my world around. I understood where I was supposed to be. Then it hit me—I was a missionary. I was spreading God everywhere I went. They didn't know it, and I didn't realize it, but I was an extension of God in my job. I truly loved my kids God had placed with me to nurture, love, and teach for many, many years.

I so enjoyed going to school every day. My devotion to my kids was genuine, true love. I fought for my kids. They needed an advocate in their lives, and God put me there for them. They needed someone to help them get from grade nine to grade twelve, and I was blessed to be able to enjoy that journey in their lives.

When I moved to Florida, the journey continued. I am now teaching middle school. My missionary work still continues. I am a teacher, but I'm also where God needs me to be. I'm still an extension of Him. When I started out, I didn't realize all of the goodness that God had planned for my life. He did, though.

Challenge: Don't ever give up on your goals. Don't let anyone tell you that you can't. You can. Your journey might take twists and turns, but in the end, you'll get there. Stay with it.

Sometimes, you need to endure rejection in order to build your self-esteem and character.

When I was growing up in church and listening to the amazing Bible stories, it made me want to be a missionary. I just knew that when I grew up, that's what I was going to do. I remember filling out the character surveys heading into high school so that I could identify my career interests and figure out what I wanted to do with my life. I wanted to be a missionary.

From a very young age, I was influenced by my older sister who was studying to be a teacher. During the summer, she would spend her breaks at home and practice on us kids. She was very patient and kind. She had a heart for the job. I wanted to be a teacher. I was debating about being a teacher and a missionary when I realized that they are sort of the same thing in a way. So I decided on teaching.

My actual student-teaching experience was quite brutal. I was paired with a third-grade class and the most energetic, spunky, smiling mentor-teacher. I knew I was in trouble. I hadn't really developed my social skills yet, so I was struggling to show my emotions for my career choice and how much I really enjoyed it. I knew I couldn't measure up to her expectations. I didn't. Upon finishing my experience, she recommended that I choose another field.

I landed my first job teaching special needs students at the elementary school in my hometown. I thought I was doing pretty well. I was making a difference and having fun. When I interviewed for the open teaching position, my principal ended the interview by saying that he didn't think I was qualified to teach. My heart broke. I remember keeping my composure and going to my room and crying. Was I really that bad?

I knew it was time to leave because I was getting nowhere and my talents were not appreciated. I was loved by my kids and parents but rejected by my boss. He even wrote me a nice reference letter to the tune of recommending that if I was going to be hired, it should be for a tutoring position and not a teaching position. I had my ways of intercepting his negativity. I applied for and got a job at a local high school. I spent fourteen years of my life teaching special needs students in all the different subject areas that high school offered. Again, I was loved by my kids and parents. I was home. I built my life around my job.

I built my character, and my self-esteem became even stronger. I enjoyed teaching. I enjoyed knowing that I had the knowledge and means to help kids be successful and productive adults. I loved them. I began coaching and advising different groups at school. My life personality flourished, and I came alive socially. I built a large extended family through school. I poured myself into my job.

When I look back at the rejection I endured by one man not once but twice, I realized that he didn't even know me. He was trying to fit me into a mold that others had fallen into in order to work for him. I wasn't hired by him, so he didn't have control. He flat out didn't like me. My evaluations were negative. He tried everything he could to discourage me. He succeeded in helping me to move on into a place where God intended for me to be for a while. God sent me where I needed to grow and flourish, and I did.

Don't ever allow someone's opinion of you to shape you. Don't let rejection rule your life. Use it as a sign that it's time to move onto something different. When a door closes, yes, find an open one, and walk through it with confidence. What do you have to lose? At least walking forward builds your confidence and character because you're trusting God to guide your steps. Don't be afraid. Step out in faith.

Challenge: Take the negative, and turn it into positive. Look for the next door to open. Walk through it.

It takes more effort to maintain a good habit than it does to drop it. Good habits are formed and take practice.

A good diet plan is changing your eating habits. It's about eating healthy foods and exercising. Staying active is part of the plan. Runners don't just get up one day and run fifteen miles; they gradually increase their stamina. Weightlifters don't just walk over to the bar and raise five hundred pounds. They have to train their body and gradually adjust. A good habit takes time, effort, and fortitude. You have to *want* to do it.

Just as amazing athletes don't just happen overnight, spiritual habits also take time. What's a spiritual habit? It might be praying, reading your Bible or devotional, spending time with God away from distractions, attending church, or even giving to others. You get to choose the habits that you want to form. No one can make you do anything unless you allow them to. You control you.

In the religious world, many habits can become demands. When I was growing up, we attended church at least one day through the week and then twice on Sunday. My parents started the habit for me at a young age. It seemed like every time something was going on at church, our family was present. We were avid supporters.

Revivals increased our time at church to every evening during the week. I remember coming home from school, getting what homework I could done, and then heading off to church. I was tired and worn out. Was the service and sermon beneficial to me? Not always. Sometimes, I was so exhausted that I wasn't really paying attention, but I was there in body. As a young kid, I remember sitting on the back pew playing paper football with my brother during the sermon. No, I didn't get much out of it.

As an adult, I got to pick and choose which habits I wanted to maintain. One of my favorite things to do is read through the Bible each year. I started doing it as a kid all on my own. It's one habit I still enjoy. It's also my quiet time every morning with God. I read through the stories and scripture, and then certain things come to light. It's almost as if when I have questions in my head, God answers them for me as I read. He helps me understand the scripture. If I really want to get a different perspective, I use my app for a different take on the scripture. I still have those aha moments of understanding after reading through the Bible about forty times.

I so enjoy my prayer time with God. It's the first thing I do after I get up in the morning. It's the last thing I do before I get into bed. Yes, I still get down on my knees to talk with God. It allows me to focus on Him and my day. In the morning, I ask for blessings on me, my friends, and my family. At night, I thank God for His blessings on me, my friends, and my family. I actually talk with God all day long. I can be driving, walking, riding my bike, exercising, and still enjoy just carrying on a conversation with Him. I practice it. Talking with God is like talking to my friend. When I feel the presence of God, I know I have His full attention.

You have the choice to maintain an amazing spiritual life, just as you do for your physical life. God doesn't change. He loves to hear from you. He enjoys when you call His name and honor Him. He is listening when you cry out for help. He's there when you need wisdom in a situation. He knows what's best for you. Develop healthy spiritual habits. Start off small, and increase as you go. Ask God to help you. He will. He enjoys your company. He's not watching to see if you fail; He's watching you succeed.

Challenge: Choose a new spiritual habit. Practice it every day. Increase your time on task little by little.

When you recognize that you can't make it on your own strength, God will strengthen you.

How many times have you been in a situation only to find yourself saying, "I can't do this anymore"? We find ourselves in that very position more often than not. Society, social media, family, jobs, and even the news darken our senses to the point where we just want to give up. Being overwhelmed can be daunting. Circumstances in our lives change. Addictions haunt us. Past memories constantly remind us of who we were rather than who we are. Life just zips by, and we find ourselves in survival mode.

I remember having an episode at school in the middle of the day. I walked into my friend's room next door, squatted down on the floor, and just began weeping. I just kept saying, "I can't take it anymore." I was escorted to the nurse's station while the counselor came and took over my class. I had been so overwhelmed by teaching, things happening in my social life, disappointment, and depression that I was done. That breaking point brought me back to reality, though. I was okay. I was just overdoing it and needed some rest too. I was exhausted mentally, physically, and emotionally.

So often, though, I've seen those who haven't recovered as well as I did. Some even to the point of suicide or hospitalization. I know that I made it through that dilemma and many more because I knew God and He had my back. What about those who don't know Him or can't rely on His strength in times of crisis? What about those who fall into addiction and journey into a downward spiral of helplessness? Who do they call on? Do they know God is there?

I have a very good support base from my family and close friends. I have people who truly care about me. Most importantly, I have God. When I find myself at the bottom and I just can't see a way out, there's always a small sliver of light that shines through the darkness. It's there; I just have to focus on it. It's there to guide me through the darkness of my dilemma and back to the light of day. I can't imagine trying to go on without the strength of God. When my strength is gone, God shows up and carries me.

I remember when the picture of the "Footprints" first came out many, many years ago. It had such a profound impact on my life. Yes, when there's been only one set of footprints, that's when Jesus carried me. He didn't leave me. He's been beside me the whole time. Sometimes, we have to go through struggles to really understand that we're not alone. My relationship with God is not one of codependency but dependency. I can't make it on my own.

When you've come through a difficult time in your life, you realize, too, that you were not alone. God allows us to go through hardships in order to build our faith and trust in Him. He doesn't cause us pain or heartache but allows us to depend on Him. Sometimes, He has to reach deeper to some in order for them to understand His love. He's not punishing us; He's loving us into another level of trust and dependency.

If you never experienced hardships or trials in your life, how would you know the goodness and love of God? He wants us to grow as Christians in order to build our faith. We have to go through things in order to grow. It would be easy if we just decided to grow our faith on our own, but that doesn't always happen. God needs to push us a little and extend our boundaries for us to really see where we are. Don't give up in the middle of a trial. Your breakthrough is a testimony. Your faith is a testimony. Your endurance is a testimony.

Challenge: Trust that God has your back. He accepts those who are burdened and stressed out. He loves you.

Some people are so deep in their comfort zone that it takes an earthquake to move them out.

Let's face it. Being comfortable in a place or position makes us feel the most confident, secure, and needed. In my comfort zone, I have built up a safe place where people are welcomed in, but I control who stays and leaves. My environment is secure, and I do a great job of maintaining my livelihood. I feel good about myself. I know the expectations. I don't experience too many surprises. I go with the flow.

In 2004, my comfort zone was upended. My environment changed quickly. Circumstances made me hate my job. A place where I had been for fourteen years suddenly became a war zone to me. I was trying to defend myself, but the outside opposition was stronger and mightier than me. I was done.

The circumstances weren't just those petty little things that irritate you. These were life-changing events. I was suspended from my job for five days. In my eyes, I had defended a family at my school and got caught in a mess between power figures. I almost got fired, so a suspension was good. Upon return, I had lost the desire to even teach at my school. The place I had spent so much time, effort, and energy on was dead to me. In the long run, all the good that I had done meant nothing. I meant nothing. It was a rude awakening.

It was a tough situation, but it clearly knocked me out of my comfort zone. My life was turned upside down. The school where I thought that I would teach forever and retire from was now my source of stress, disappointment, and anger. I finished the last three months of that school year on medical leave.

While I was on medical leave, I had a chance to reevaluate my life. I had been so busy with school and teaching that I never really thought about myself or where I was going. I was almost forty-five years old when I decided I was going to move far away. With my resume, surely, I could land a teaching job fairly easily.

I did. I moved to Florida within five months. I didn't really know anyone. I had family in St. Petersburg and Lakeland, but none was in close proximity. I left all of my family and friends in Ohio. I didn't realize it at the time, but God had a different plan for my life. It took the turmoil, mental anguish, and emotional stress just for Him to get my attention. I was on my own. I had no one to run to except God. I had no one to hang out with except God. I was starting over. I felt free. Yes, I was a little scared, but God worked everything out in my favor. It didn't matter that it took a major pay cut; I was going to the happiest place on earth!

I succeeded. I made new friends. I had an extended family. Everyone was so nice and inviting to me. I loved my new school. It was middle school, but I adapted pretty quickly. I made it through the culture shock. God blessed me every single day. I enjoyed teaching again. I loved my kids. I enjoyed being at school. I enjoyed God. It was like a new friendship with Him alone had developed. I had to learn to trust Him.

Going out of your comfort zone doesn't take a big move. Some people like me, though, depend on that safe space to control their everyday life. Their routines become established. It's easy to get lost in the crowd. For those of us who are controlling and cautious, it might take an earthquake to move us. Sometimes, God goes to great lengths to get your attention. He gives you little clues and hints along the way, but then He has to bring out the heavy artillery.

All God ever wants is what's best for you. You have to step out on faith and depend on Him. He has your best interests at heart. He will take care of you. He can make the move gradual or big. It's your choice. God has so much more for you to do outside of yourself and zone of proximity. Trust Him and trust yourself.

Challenge: Step out in faith. Ask God what it is you need to be doing. He's got a plan for you. Step into it.

You can't be owned unless you let someone own you.

I am the kind of person who absorbs people's emotions and feelings around me. I am a good listener. When someone is in need, I am a giver. It's a gift. All my life I have been a pleaser. It's a good quality to have unless it overtakes your life. I have had friends who have taken advantage of my good nature and sensitivity in the past, so much so that I suffered physically and mentally.

As a kid, I learned not to mess up because I would get yelled at by my parents. I knew that if I did what was right, I didn't have to deal with the feeling of failure. I hated disappointing others. I learned to do any job with accuracy, precision, and expertise. I will tell you that I am a lifelong learner and very book smart. Sometimes, I don't have common sense. I still get reminded of it as an adult. If there's an easy way to do something, I don't know about it. I do things how it makes sense to me and use my available resources. Then someone shows me an easier way. I see it as my personal disability, but I've learned to live with it. I'm good.

People don't understand the stress of what it takes for me to complete a task sometimes. I am methodical in my thinking processes, and I do read the instructions on how to put shelves together. I get anxious if a screw is left over and it's not supposed to be. I am adventurous on my own, but when it comes to thinking of others, I care about their emotions and safety.

As an adult, I had a friend who used me to a point that I felt like my job was in jeopardy. I allowed this person to control me. I was old enough to know that it was wrong but also felt an obligation to the family and the kids caught in a mess. I was their stability. I was the stand-in mom. I didn't want to be, but it happened. It was the first time I began dealing with depression and anxiety. I really didn't know what it was but understood pretty quickly. I was not in control of my own life. I was in fear that I would somehow lose my job. That scared me the most because all I had was me.

I began having panic attacks. The first one was in a restaurant while waiting for my food to be served. The sudden feeling of losing control came over me. I remember walking outside around the building several times to lower my heart rate and get myself under control. I thought it was all of the coffee I was drinking at work. I stopped drinking coffee cold turkey. The panic attacks didn't go away. They were happening more frequently to the point that I went to every doctor possible to rule out things and help me get better. I ended up on medication and seeing a psychiatrist on a regular basis. I was getting it under control. I was feeling better about myself. I moved out on my own again and lowered my stress levels.

Once I moved out, I realized that I allowed myself to be in the depressing situation I was in. I allowed my mental and emotional states to be compromised. I was on a new journey of finding myself and taking care of myself all over again. More than once, I contemplated suicide. It wasn't the coffee; it was all of the situations all my life that I allowed control over me. I was under continuous bondage, and the load got heavier and heavier. I didn't see a way out.

People choose to control others in different ways. It can be emotional, mental, physical, sexual, and even spiritual. How many cults have been successful because of control? How many people have died spiritually, physically, and even emotionally because of someone else's control? At some point, I had to take back control and get back to God. The same goes for you. Fight back for your own sake. Stand up for you. No one deserves to be punished and controlled by another. Let them go. Take your life back. Live and be free!

Challenge: Recognize that you lost control. Get control back. Make the necessary changes to save yourself. No one else will do it for you. Let God be in control of your life.

What we value most is what changes our lives.

Have you noticed how your value system changes as you age? As a kid, I was always active, having fun, playing outside, and didn't have a care in the world. My family took care of and watched out for me. As a preteen, I became very self-conscious of what others thought about me. I thought I was a homely kid. I was a tomboy, so I didn't have time for girly stuff. I was a very good athlete and worried more about what the boys in the neighborhood thought of me than the girls. I had something to prove. I hated to lose. I wanted to be the best at whatever I did.

As a teenager, my focus became my church. I was into sports, but when I felt the call to be devoted to my church, sports got trumped. My academics in high school were always first and foremost. I was a pleaser, so I worried more about helping others be happy and less about me. What I valued most was not the church or the religion, or even God, but those who influenced me most at the time. I supported my pastoral family with all my heart. I believed they were seriously close to God. My focus became their well-being.

Pleasing others sucked the life out of me. Every waking moment was making sure others were taken care of, and my life didn't matter. My life was put on a drastic hold. I was so devoted that my mental health became compromised. My physical stamina slowed down. I lived for others, not God. I thought I was serving God but came to realize later that my good will was taken advantage of. My mental health diminished even more.

As a young adult, I was influenced into thinking that my life revolved around the church and religion. My sole purpose in life was to make sure that my pastoral family was taken care of and my church was a beacon in the community. Again, I was physically worn out from trying to do too many things at the same time. I had my own juggling act going on. All the while I was teaching full-time, coaching, and taking on extra jobs at my school. The same devotion I had for my church was also there for my job. I absolutely loved teaching and coaching. I had been burned out at church for years but didn't know how to say no without feeling afraid of offending someone, especially my pastoral family.

I wasn't happy with what I was doing at church. I was asked to take on more and more, and my personal self gradually slipped away. I did my "good works" out of devotion to people, not God. When I had my epiphany that God loved me, everything changed. By that time, my pastoral family had moved on, and I left the only church I knew from childhood and the city where I grew up. I was on my own. Those I allowed to control my life gradually lost their grip. I was becoming more independent and centered on my personal health. It was a real struggle. My values changed to God and me.

It's pretty amazing how my eyes were opened in a moment of time. God showed me the reality of my situation. I had been so caught up in pleasing others that I hardly even knew how to make decisions and think for myself. I never had to. My life didn't matter. Pleasing others did. When my focus changed to God, my values changed. I lived to serve Him and no one else. I had more freedom in my life than I ever thought possible. My physical health changed, and I had to begin the journey of working on my mental health. When my focus changed to God, my value system changed. I became healthier mentally, physically, emotionally, and spiritually. God just patiently waited for me to get there. I made it.

Challenge: Love yourself. Focus on God. Listen for His voice. Don't be influenced by anything but God.

God is love. If you believe in God, you will love others.

One of the greatest examples of God's love is Mother Teresa. Her journey into the streets of Calcutta began with helping the sick and less fortunate. She is an amazing example of what God intended for the human race to be. Mother Teresa loved unconditionally, helped without asking, and healed as many as she could. All the while, she was teaching about Jesus.

Think about the story in the New Testament about the Good Samaritan. The Samaritans were looked upon as the lower class in their country. They had a reputation of being outcasts. When the Samaritan took care of the man in need on the side of the road, it showed the true love of God. The Samaritan saw someone in need and came to his rescue. Can you imagine being that servant whom Jesus spoke about in his parables? He was honored because of his actions. He expected nothing in return. He is still honored today and revered as an example of what God's love truly is.

I never really understood the true love of God until I was in my thirties. I had been told that God loved me but also believed that my good works earned His love. While I was driving home one day, the thought hit me. God loves me not because of what I do but because I'm His. He loves me for me. God created me to talk with Him and have a relationship with Him. He loves me unconditionally with nothing in return. He loves me when I mess up and fall down. He loves me when I break under temptations. He longs to hear my voice and spend time with me. I imagined Him looking down on me with the most loving, caring eyes of affection.

It was an epiphany. I had served God all my life and never understood His love. Once I did, I truly saw the meaning of loving others. It brought a genuine smile to my face. It brought a bounce to my step. I then realized that loving others was an extension of God. My whole demeanor changed. At that point, I didn't care what others thought. I was God's child, and all I wanted to do was please Him. It was a breakthrough for me.

Seeing others through God's eyes was a whole different world. I truly understood. I had more self-confidence. My faith began to grow even more. My desire to seek God's face, to pray, and to talk with Him was something new. I was in awe. I genuinely praised and worshiped Him from my heart and soul. I loved God back. It was nothing like I had been taught growing up.

God began placing individuals in my path to love also. I did the best I could. I remember seeing panhandlers on the side of the road asking for help during the holiday season. I bought a ton of groceries and dropped them off for the family. While others were passing by him, I was impressed to show God. That happened many times over. Simple tasks became conversations about God. I was where I needed to be.

God placed kids into my classes that needed Him too. The opportunities kept coming. I reached out to as many as He would let me. Even when I wasn't earning much as a teacher, much of my paycheck was spent on helping out my less fortunate students. I could never outgive God either. I prayed for those around me. I loved on those in my reach. I had a very hard time turning anyone away. God blessed me back.

Give until you can't. Love because of God. See others through God's eyes. Pray that God will use you to help others, and He will. Just be ready because you will be an extension of His love too.

Challenge: Love others. Draw close to God so you can truly know His love for you.

It takes more effort to be negative and hurtful than it does to be kind and giving.

I'm a giving person by nature. I enjoy blessing others. God has blessed me, so I enjoy passing on the wealth. Sometimes, God sneaks in a blessing to me through others. I don't like surprises, but good words get to my heart. I'm always looking for God in every situation. I know my path crosses individuals every single day that were not a mistake. God places people in my life for a reason. God places my students in my classes for a reason. In my heart, I feel God, so I know it's just Him being good to me.

One day, I was walking into the store. Without thinking about it, I was on a mission with a list of items in my hand. Usually, I'm compelled to get in and out of the store quickly because I am not a shopper. I was almost to the door when I locked eyes with a gentleman walking to his car. He looked at me, pointed up to the sky, and said, "Look up! Isn't the sun beautiful?" He kept walking. I stopped and looked up at the beautiful sun shining all around us. It was beautiful outside. Then I paused and thought about what he said.

I looked around and saw the beauty. In my spiritual self, I heard, "Look up! Isn't the Son beautiful?" I smiled to myself and felt God where I was standing. That special moment in time took no more than seconds of my life. It made me take notice of Jesus and His beauty. I just grinned because God had sent someone in my path to bless me. Who knows? It could have been an angel. Yes, I was surprised but delightfully so.

Being kind doesn't take effort. I have been asked for money by individuals while walking into a store. If I have it, I give it with a "God bless you." I have been in restaurants where I've felt like paying for a stranger's dinner and I got their check and paid for it. I was walking out of a store and gave a gentleman bungee cords to hold down a mattress he was hauling home. I have watched someone's groceries while they went to get their car in the rain. I have helped short people get items in the grocery store off the top shelf. I have paid for people's food or gas because they were just a little short and in need. I have learned to be ready and be kind.

I've also had my negative moments. I've had people irritate me to the point where I've lost sleep or dreamed about getting revenge on them. I have had people talk behind my back, and I pondered for days on how I could get them back. I have had people use me to the point where my life was disrupted for weeks, months, or years. I've had people say things about me to my face, and then I tried to make a move to avoid confrontation with them. I've had jealousy eat away at me for weeks over stupid things. I have taken time to plot defense against those who hurt me. Sometimes, it took days or weeks of my life.

Acts of kindness are fleeting moments and not stressful. My heart feels joyful. Acts of revenge make me angry and take days, months, or years of my life. Being negative and planning an action take up so much time. The plotting and calculations are innumerable. The scenarios that run through my head have to be just right to get the right effect. My heart feels horrible. In essence, I should have given my worries and concerns to God. God says that vengeance is His. I'm not sure why I don't just let Him get back at people for me. Actually, some call it karma. I call it God's revenge. When God says He's going to take care of it, He does.

As a teenager, I had to learn hard lessons with my attitude. It wasn't pleasant all the time. I learned to pray and ask God to help me. I didn't want to be negative or vengeful. As an adult, I have learned to give things to God. What I can't control shouldn't worry me. I'm taking years off my own life because of someone else. I'm not looking out for me or being fair to myself. I don't want to waste my life on making someone else miserable. I choose life. I'm trusting God more than I ever have. He knows what we go through. He's always got our back. He also wants us to learn to depend on Him.

Challenge: Choose kindness over revenge. Nothing negative is worth losing precious moments of your life.

The fear of the unknown can be crippling. Jesus took away our fear. He came to give us life and hope.

If you think about it, we live in a society that promotes more fear than good. When I was growing up in school, we lived life the best we knew how. If someone had anxiety or fears, or even mental health issues, no one really talked about it. We accepted everyone for who they were, and life went on. I can barely remember even having students in special needs classes. It seemed like we were all put into the regular population to figure out life. We learned to help one another. We learned to support those in need. We learned that we were different, but we had each other. We, as kids, learned to live together no matter what differences we had.

As a teacher, I have noticed within the last few years the increasing number of kids who were crippled by anxiety, depression, the future, abuse, learning disabilities, bullying, and many more mental health issues than ever before. We have so many students on learning plans, special programs, behavior plans, mental health plans, plans for attention problems, and even plans for medical issues related to learning. The fears these kids live with on a daily basis have to be daunting. Some have a fear of coming to school. It's overwhelming to think of all that surrounds us when we're simply trying to educate children.

One of my greatest fears is that of the unknown. Because I like to live with a "heads up" mentality, I would rather be looking ahead to prepare what is coming at me. I don't like not knowing the outcome. I hated science class in school when I had to do experiments and hypothesize about the outcome. It drove me nuts! I didn't want to find out what *might* happen; I wanted to know a concrete answer to the problem. I'm so fortunate I didn't have to take chemistry. That would have been a nightmare in itself.

I sincerely am afraid of very deep water. Maybe I watched one too many movies about sharks when I was younger, but the seed certainly was planted. If I can't see what's under me, I don't want to be there. I love my routines. I am very good at forming habits. It's how I roll. Keep my feet on the shore, and I'm great at the ocean.

Think about the fears and phobias that people are now diagnosed with on a regular basis. It's crippling. How did our lives become so overtaken with fear? When Jesus came to us, He actually took away fear. He holds all power to overcome fear. When we trust in Him, we have no reason to fear anything. God is always in control. Sometimes, however, it's hard to truly trust in God. Fear is one great chain that holds some people captive. We have to consciously break the chain and trust God.

If fear were a tangible item, it would be easier to conquer it. Because it's such a useful vice of the enemy, it's a difficult thing for us to deal with. We have to learn that Jesus overcame Satan and all that he throws at us. Jesus is our spiritual shield and protector. When fear tries to grip us, we have to consciously pray and ask God to take over. God rolls up His sleeves and steps in. All we have to do is ask for help. We have to remember that we have no fear in Jesus Christ, who has already saved us.

I've had to deal with kids who have anxiety. Since I have issues myself, it's easy for me to walk them through attacks. It's still so very hard to watch them struggle with being in an uncomfortable place and dealing with something so large that no one understands. It breaks my heart. Mental illness is very real. Whether we were born with it or acquired it, it can be a struggle. We can overcome our adversity, though. It's not impossible. Having God surely helps. It takes trusting the God of the universe to help you in your distress. He's there. When no one else understands, He does. He has control of our fears…always.

Challenge: What fears do you face? Identify them. Face them. Give them to God. Let Him deal with them.

Just as we take care of our physical self, we should also cleanse our spiritual self. It's spiritual hygiene.

It's very difficult to teach middle school students about the importance of physical hygiene. You would think that it's a natural thing for them to want to smell nice. The problem is that they have been the way they are for so long that they are familiar and comfortable with their own smell. They don't recognize that they stink. They are kids going through puberty. We've all been there. Surely, you think they would understand the importance of soap and water. For some, it's nonexistent. Others just cover it up with cologne.

I had a student who truly emitted a foul odor. Part of it was from the home. Certain smells like smoke or animals weren't his fault. It could have been that he wasn't even aware of the odor because that was his environment. It was obvious that kids couldn't handle being around him. The problem was how to make it better. I felt really badly for the kid. He just had such a nasty combination of smells on him that made you want to puke.

I decided to try something. I called the mom with a plan. I bought the kid some clothes for school. All he had to do was change into the school clothes every morning when he got on campus. He could then smell fresh, and kids could be more receptive to him. At the end of the day, he could change back into his home clothes and go home. I would bag up his clothes once a week and take them home to wash them. It worked perfectly, and the mom was okay with it, and the kid became more popular.

Just as we practice physical hygiene, we also need to practice spiritual hygiene. Have you ever been checked by something you said or did that another person called you out on? Have you ever been in a situation where all you're thinking about is how you got there? When you felt uncomfortable being in a certain place, why was that? This all goes back to the spirit of God leading you.

If you're not being checked by the spirit of God, then maybe you need a spiritual tune-up. Many times, we get comfortable in our surroundings so that we don't question whether it's a good or bad situation. We feel bold enough to go where we shouldn't and think it's okay without second-guessing our witness to others. There may be times when you try something new and don't second-guess who's watching your walk with God. We forego God's guidance and slip back into what feels good. We've lost our witness.

Spiritual hygiene is getting back to God and being led by the Spirit. Listening to that voice that says, "You probably shouldn't be doing this," would normally be enough to save you. We choose to listen less and walk farther away from God. The spirit of God doesn't leave us. He's still there trying to guide us. We need to renew our connections. We are a reflection of God. If our spiritual life is lacking, it's pretty obvious to those around us. If they are questioning our actions before we do, then we have a disconnect.

We can't be effective in leading others if our spiritual life is in need of cleansing. How do we do that? Get back to the basics of talking with and trusting God. Rely on the spirit of God to lead us. Listen to God and take His direction. Spend time in prayer for guidance and spiritual direction. Follow God's lead. Check yourself to see if what you're doing is acceptable to God. Reflect on your steps to see if you are making progress toward leading others to God.

If you're not making an impact on leading others to God, then turn it around. Get rid of the things that are weighing you down. Get close to God. Get renewed and spiritually refreshed. Get clean.

Challenge: Examine your walk. Do you hear the spirit of God leading you?

When you experience the unexpected, it can be tough to deal with. Having God makes it easier to endure.

I am a firm follower of those who sincerely do not like to be surprised. My routines mean a lot to me as I get older. To know me is to love me. I'm the whole package. I'm not avidly consumed by routines; I just like to plan ahead sometimes and know what's coming at me. I've learned to live with myself.

The worst unexpected tragedy happened a couple of years ago. I had spent several weeks with my family in Ohio and was looking forward to getting back into teaching the school year. I was rested, I had new ideas of what I wanted to do in the classroom, and I just knew that my kids were going to love what I planned for them. My family is a great resource of ideas and helping me decorate my classroom. I am blessed.

I began driving the sixteen-hour trip in one shot because it became difficult to pack and unpack my three cats on the long journey. Once we get on the road, we just keep pressing forward. Leaving in the early afternoon allows us to drive through the night with less traffic. I'm able to make better time driving at night. My sister usually flies to my state and rides to Ohio with me. My niece usually rides home with me and then flies back to Ohio. I so look forward to quality time with both. My cats have made the trip several times; they are really good travelers.

We had left on a Sunday morning and headed back home. The traffic wasn't bad, I didn't receive a speeding ticket, and we laughed and were having a good time, hoping to make it all the way. We were about forty-five minutes from home when the unexpected happened. A speeding car was coming up on my rear really quickly. I thought it was a cop, but I was only doing seventy, so I couldn't figure out what was going on. The car came faster. I thought it was going to suddenly slow down. It plowed into my rear end without braking, going about ninety miles per hour.

I couldn't react quickly enough to let my niece even know what was coming. The impact launched my car off the pavement. We landed, and I gained control and steered the car over to the side of the road. I was in shock. The other car was a mess too. I didn't know if anyone was dead. Two of my cats ended up in the dash window, scared beyond words. My niece was belted in and okay, with one of my cats under her feet. We were all okay. Shaken up, but we were okay. Miraculously, the driver in the other car was okay too. It was four in the morning. We waited until seven to finally get towed away. I was a mess.

The next few months were very difficult. I had to start school. During preplanning, my cat Sam had to be put down. He was supposed to live to my retirement. My other cat, Beaumont, had to be put down a month later from complications. I was struggling every single day to survive. My new car was broken into and stuff stolen. It seemed like it was one thing after another. I never really got my footing until January.

I was sitting in church one Sunday during this time, and God spoke to me. I had been thinking about the accident and why it all happened. He told me that He knew it was going to happen when I left Ohio. He was protecting me the best He could. He reassured me that He was with me and was taking care of me. I just sobbed. My heart had been ripped out, and I was trying to heal. Those simple words gave me peace.

After all of the formalities were over, I wrote a letter to the young lady who had torn my life apart. I told her that I forgave her and probably saved her life by being in the way. I told her about Jesus and hoped someday she would know Him. I recovered physically, mentally, and emotionally after several months. Without God, I don't think I would have made it on my own. He was my anchor through it all.

Challenge: No matter how hard you try, you can't avoid the unexpected. Hold on to God when it happens.

At some point, you have to leave a crippling past to move forward. Sometimes, that includes people.

One of the most difficult things in a situation is dealing with people's emotions. I am one who has always considered others before myself. I always try to please people so that they are not uncomfortable. If something bad happens in a relationship, I always take the blame upon myself. Everything, it seems, is always my fault for some reason. As I grew older and wiser, I learned that I didn't need to apologize for things I didn't do. I was a scapegoat for others. I was dependent on others, so keeping a solid relationship was emotionally and mentally important to me. I was not always at fault; I was human. I was being used.

I had allowed relationships to drain me. I didn't exist, because I lost myself somewhere in the mess. On the outside, I was great. On the inside, I wanted to die. I allowed people to use me to their advantage and was scared to death that if I ended the relationship, I would struggle being alone. This is hard to believe coming from someone who grew up with sixteen older brothers and sisters. I had depended on people all my life.

As an adult, nothing changed. I hadn't learned how to stand on my own two feet. I was sucked into a life of servitude under the guise of religion. I learned that God didn't want me the way I was. He didn't ask for me to give so much of myself and my time that I was exhausted and burned out. He didn't expect me to wear myself down for the sake of others. I know He was trying to help me grow; it just took a longer time than expected. I can imagine Him looking at me sometimes and smacking His head.

My life had been infused into a very volatile relationship during my teen years. I didn't understand it at the time, because I was seeking God and thought it was what I was supposed to be doing. I had blinders on and dared not get off my path or switch lanes. I stood up for what I believed, even though it was wrong many times. I supported what I thought was right, even though it wasn't. I didn't see it. It was unhealthy.

In my head, I had grand illusions of what I thought life was going to be like. I really believed that I was doing the right thing and couldn't figure out why things weren't working out in my direction. God was smacking His head and trying to get my attention. I was a fighter. When door after door closed, I was done.

I moved a thousand miles away and broke off the dependent relationship I had known for over twenty years. My whole life was turned upside down. It was hurtful. I poured out my heart on paper because I knew that in person my voice wouldn't be heard. It hadn't in the past. I was brutally honest and called things as they were. Years of hurt, anger, disappointment, and mistrust spewed out of me. I took several days to write down my feelings. That was a lot of ground to cover. Most people say, "Write down your feelings, but don't mail the letter." I did. If I took all that time to unload, it was going to hit its mark.

My last words were, "I will probably never hear from you again." I didn't. All those years that I poured myself into a relationship were gone in a second. I realized that none of it truly mattered. I had been used and misled into thinking that I was something important. I had been scammed into thinking that I was loved, when I wasn't. I was only good for what needed to be done at the time. God got me. He helped me understand.

It took a while to rid myself of that past experience because it was so deeply rooted inside me. Everything about me was wrapped up in it. I was a pawn in a chess game. I was replaced and put aside like a used rag. My eyes were truly opened. From it, however, I have been able to help others heal. God knew what He was doing. I was too stubborn to listen.

Challenge: Revisit relationships. Get out of the negative ones that suck the life out of you.

The uncertainty of your future can be scary when it's in the hands of people. With God, it's under control.

We all have those days when everything is going well and then something so unbelievable happens that it throws you into a tailspin. How do you handle it? How do you deal with the fear and uncertainty? People are watching your response. As a Christian, you have to get to the point that your faith is stable and God is real, even through the trials of life. People who don't know God respond differently. You have to show God in every circumstance. That's your testimony. God allows us to go through things to learn.

It was a typical school day, and we were preparing for a special breakfast to honor the kids who had performed well for the quarter. I was busy orchestrating everything and helping set up. We had been planning this day in advance, so we were excited about honoring our students. I was in charge of the parent committee, so I had lots of friends there helping out.

I turned around at one point to gauge our progress when I was summoned into the main office. I walked into the conference room only to be greeted by the superintendent, the principal, and the treasurer of the school. I thought they were excited about our breakfast and had come to participate. On the contrary, I was given a letter of reprimand and advised that at the next meeting I should have union representation. Immediate panic set it. What had been a happy day just went south really fast. I was in shock.

I contacted my union representative and prepared for my meeting. I was being charged with items A through M. I was advised on what to do. My friend who was a union rep told me that once the board has it out for you, you're done. I had poured my life into my school. I was in total shock. I didn't know which way to turn. My whole life had been turned upside down in a split second. I was scared. I admit it.

I had been helping my kids participate in the special testing of the ACT, which is a college entrance test. My students had special testing accommodations, and I had been the supervisor through the school for over five years. One parent had come to me to try to help them navigate through the system. I gladly obliged and went to it. Because of that action, I was going to be terminated.

The meeting took place. I had already been threatened by my principal about my actions and reactions, but no one heard that part. It was her word against mine. She couldn't understand why I wasn't taking responsibility for fraudulently participating in the special testing when I didn't do anything wrong. If it had been fraudulent, why didn't the ACT board call me to question? She took every opportunity to turn on me. I was trying to figure things out but not getting anywhere. At that point, I thought I was done.

The meeting was over. I received five days of suspension without pay. They were actually trying to fire me. Honestly, there was more going on in this situation that was brought to light, but no one admitted it. I took the fall. I took my suspension. My response was one of "I'm done here." I couldn't handle the constant nagging by my principal and her watching my every move. I took the rest of the year off. It was February.

During my time off, I healed and recovered. I learned how the system worked. I wasn't bitter but decided to move my life in a new direction. I was hired over the phone by a principal in Florida. Best move of my life. I got everything in order and took off not knowing anyone there. I had a sense of peace. I know I have done my job. God was moving me in a different direction. It was a big move but much needed. He was in control of the entire situation. I was more disappointed by the actions of others than I was myself. In the end, it didn't really matter. God had my back. Doors opened. My career flourished, and I found myself.

Challenge: Check to see who's in control. If it's God, don't worry. Feel the pain, and then move on.

If not God, then who? If not God, then what?

When I moved to my new location in life, God has placed me in the midst of those who may not believe in God. This situation perplexes me because I grew up in a small town where pretty much everyone went to church and believed in God. If you claimed to be an atheist, there was almost nothing short of holding a God Squad intervention to introduce you to the one true God and help you understand the significance of His existence. No, that never really happened, but there were people who nag others to death until they wore them down to Christianity. They eventually saw the errors of their ways. Praying Christians can do a lot.

So in my current situation, I have friends who are agnostics, atheists, idol worshippers, and simply believers that Jesus was a regular prophet in history like all the others. It makes me cringe to think that they wake up every single day, see the beauty all around them, and not believe that God had something to do with it all. I realize that they believe the way they do for a reason, I just don't get it.

My beautiful friends are in positions of authority and have the ability to influence others. They are amazing individuals and so fun to be around. I just watch them and think that they are so happy, but they are also missing out on so much more because they don't really know and understand God. I guess I've never thought about worshiping another god or not ever believing that God didn't exist. He's just been such a big part of my life for so many years. To think that Jesus died on a Cross without having a connection or a special relationship with God the Father seems unfathomable to me.

Every day when I wake up, I have a joy like no other. If I didn't believe in God, who or what would I put my trust in? What would I attribute to the beauty around me or the breath of life that I've been given? If I didn't know that someday when I die and had no hope of an eternal life in heaven, what value would I put on my own? Simply, I can't believe an existence without God. If I had no hope that I am where I am and who I am by God's design, what would my life be lived for? Would I just be going through the motions of this life?

I would find it difficult to believe that I have no purpose in life. What reason would I have for getting out of bed every morning? What would be my motivation to exist if I didn't know God or believe that He has my life in His hands? I know I would be completely lost. Who would hold me accountable for how I live my life? Who would set the positive ground rules for me to live by? Who would love me unconditionally as God has? Who could I depend on when no one else is around if not God?

People exist in my life to keep me straight and grounded. God exists in my life to keep me spiritually grounded and balanced. My faith and trust in the one who made the universe according to the Bible are my entire world. The faith I have in humans is nowhere near the trust and faith I have in God. I find it difficult to believe that people can fill their lives with someone or something that doesn't respond to them. God is quick to answer and provides for my needs on a daily basis. What other god does that?

I love my friends. I love that they are successful and they prosper. I just wish they could know and understand God like I do. I try my best to lead others to Him. To me, it's not a chore. I want them to understand His goodness and help give them hope that He is real. I want them to feel the presence of God as I do anytime and anywhere. He's not in a box or left at home for me to visit when I want to. He goes with me always. I am reminded of Him in everything. I exist because of Him. I can't imagine living life without Him.

Challenge: Take a step back and figure out your true beliefs. Is God the center of your focus, or a god the center of your life? If not God, then what is so captivating?

Your freedom depends on you. Don't get comfortable in your own prison. Break the cycle.

Have you ever wondered why some people can't manage to leave an abusive situation? It blows my mind that they can be so caught up and blinded by someone who mistreats them and abuses them. It's so very sad to watch them struggle under the weight of oppression because they may not see a way out. Their lives completely change into something unrecognizable because they've lost their identity.

I'm sure I'm not the only one who has struggled with helping someone in an abusive circumstance. Adults can handle most things, but when children are affected, something just tugs at your heart to do something. Kids don't ask for the situations they're born into. They don't get to choose their families or parents. They are given what they get. Hopefully parents grow up and understand their responsibility of bringing a delicate life into this world.

I have a very close friend who struggled with spousal abuse. It had happened more than once where she was so beaten down that she just simply existed without a fight. She lived under the terror that every evening when she went home, the unexpected would happen and it may be her last drive home. She lived her life in total submission to someone who physically, mentally, and emotionally abused her. She was such an intelligent individual, too, with college degrees and recognizable certifications.

God sent me into her life in a roundabout way. I never thought we would become friends, but it turned out that she was so much fun to hang out with and had an awesome sense of humor…like mine. We hit it off. She was in a bad situation and tried to cover up her scars of pain. Mostly, she maintained a superficial relationship with people but never really expressed her true feelings. Then she became pregnant.

In an abusive situation, what should have been the happiest moment of her life turned into protective custody. She carried the baby to full term and delivered him into the world. Her entire attention was focused on protecting the baby instead of herself. She put herself between the baby and her spouse. Her life saved his. She was a very good mother and protected her little guy like no other. He truly was a beautiful blessing from God. I had a front-row seat to the entire situation. I didn't mind, because I felt that I was supposed to be there to help her out. I had never experienced this before, so I prayed and sincerely asked God to intervene.

To me, it was a dire situation. I watched my friend struggle to maintain sanity in her life of upheaval. So many things happened that I had no control of. I couldn't just intervene, so I prayed and encouraged her to make the right moves so that she and the baby would be protected. It was tough. The decisions that she had to make were unbelievable. She was so scared and afraid but did her best to survive.

Eventually, the spouse lost contact and wasn't really around anymore. I tried to comfort her as she took on all of the jobs that she had never done before while being both a mom and a dad to her son. She had it tough. She cried, went through depressions, felt guilty, and probably wanted to die. She had her son to live for. My feelings of inadequacy just mounted. I couldn't understand how she chose time after time to stay in the prison she was in. It's so hard to look beyond your circumstances to focus on anything better when you've been beaten down so badly.

She survived and even made a clean break from her spouse. Her life turned around. her confidence soared. She was an entirely new person. Finally, she broke the cycle and was able to stand on her own two feet. It was tough, but she managed to save herself. I believe God saved her life. I was there to help.

Challenge: Break free from what or who imprisons you. You have the ability to stop the cycle. Be free.

The most difficult part of a friendship is watching someone go through something you can't do anything about. You give them to God.

I have always heard that God allows certain people to come into your life for a reason. As I grew older, I realized it was true. Those who have passed through my life have taught me lifelong lessons. Some have been positive, and others negative. Either way, I have learned. God has shown me the highs and lows of being a true friend. How I choose to accept my lessons is up to me.

When I moved over a thousand miles away from my family, I was on a new adventure. It was just me and God. I felt free for once in my life. I settled in pretty quickly to my new surroundings and made friends easily. God knew who I needed and began moving my life like a chessboard. Strategic moves allowed me to extend my family and gather friends.

In a new school district, I was responsible for specific classes to train me how to teach. I signed up and worked to get them out of the way. In one of my classes, I met a good friend Michelle. We were about the same age, she taught kindergarten, and we both had positive fun-loving attitudes. We immediately hit it off. We signed up for the same classes and became fast friends. We made the time go quickly in classes by laughing and having fun. God brought us together.

One day, I received a call that Michelle was in the hospital because she had fallen in her garage. She went to get her seriously bruised breast examined only to find that she had cancer. I was shaken. I rushed to the hospital after school and was there when the doctor came in to explain the severity of her condition. It didn't look good. Not only did she have breast cancer, but it was in other parts of her body that were hard to heal. The doctor left. Michelle, her husband, and I prayed for God to take care of things.

Michelle didn't get a good prognosis, and every test pointed to the worst possible scenario. Things weren't going how we planned. She underwent surgeries, chemotherapy, and radiation, and did everything the doctors told her to do. Michelle lost her ability to work full-time and eventually had to quit her passion…teaching. She went through all of the reactions to medication. Her immune system was compromised, she lost her hair, and her strength was fading. I would go and sit with her for hours and sometimes nights while her husband took a break. I watched her slowly fading.

Michelle lived several years after her diagnosis. Eventually, nothing else could be done, and she was losing her battle. She still kept her sense of humor. She loved life. She never let on that she was hurting. Her memory began to fade as the cancer spread to her brain. Michelle didn't have the strength to get out of bed. She had fought hard for years. She was ready to meet Jesus. I kept praying and hoping God would perform a miracle. It was so hard to have hope when my friend was dying. I laughed with her, fed her, told her school stories, and kept her company until the end. I loved my friend. I never cried in front of her.

Watching my friend go through something as terrible as cancer was one of the most difficult things in my life. I waited for a miracle. My heart was broken. Not being able to rescue her or heal her was devastating. I sat by helplessly, praying for God to ease her pain. He did. Eventually, I lost her. My heart broke when I got the call. Even though I was expecting it, I was hurting. She took a part of me with her.

When God places people in your path, it's for a reason. Some lessons are difficult, but you have to trust that God is in control. Don't stop praying and believing. Hold on for a miracle. It might come.

Challenge: Love and cherish those God places in your path. They're there for a reason.

Those who follow you are more important than those who lead you.

Growing up, I definitely was a follower. I had sixteen siblings older than me, so I was always next in line. I wasn't allowed to be a leader. I was the baby of the family. Sometimes, I got lost in the shuffle, so I'm pretty sure my opinion didn't count for much either. I sided with whoever was going to be nice to me.

As an adult, I developed into a natural leader. I was the silent leader. I had the personality, wit, and character that allowed me to bring people in close and make them feel comfortable. Being a teacher helped me perfect my skills because of getting my kids to buy into what I was teaching. They loved being in my class.

Later in my teaching career, I went back to school and earned a master's degree in education administration. Since I was doing so well as a teacher, I thought maybe I could influence and lead adults too. My degree didn't really matter in my family; I was still the baby, and my opinion didn't matter. I was having so much fun teaching at the high school level. Surely dealing with adults couldn't be that bad, right? Wrong.

Once I was trained how to deal with adults and be an effective educational leader, I looked for those qualities in my leaders. It was one of the worst things that could have happened. I began looking at how my leaders measured up to what I had been taught. It didn't go well all of the time. I became more critical and couldn't figure out why they weren't doing what we were taught to do as administrative leaders.

It changed my perspective. When I moved to Florida, I went through the leadership program for the county. I interviewed and was placed into the assistant principal pool. Let's just say I swam for a while during the time I was still trying to figure out how my leaders could be so different from what I learned. I realized that I couldn't play the game and decided to jump out of the pool. My eyes were opened. I realized that being in the classroom was way more important as a leader than being in an administrative position.

I've had the opportunity to work with and lead some of the greatest educators. These followers allowed me to help them, show them, teach them, and guide them into a positive educator role. I learned that my influence on them was what really mattered. I taught them how to have fun and to also be leaders and role models for their students. To me, that was the best lesson ever. I didn't really have anyone help me with that as a young educator; I had to learn it on my own.

I think about the thousands of kids who sat in my classes over the years. Was I the best influence and role model for them? Did I show them how to positively lead others? Did I take enough time to listen to them and help them with situations that seemed monumental to them at the time? Did they know that I truly cared for and loved them? These are some of the best qualities of a good leader. They don't just happen overnight, and they can always be perfected.

At the end of the day, did I do enough to help support those around me? Did I positively influence their life in some way? It doesn't matter how leaders lead me. If I don't agree, I can change my path. I look to my leaders as positive role models. If they don't have it, I don't follow. I can influence those who follow me, though. We are taught to lead by example.

If I can't be the best example of God, then my efforts go unnoticed. I pray every single day to do my best and to be a good person. I learn something new every day. Even at my age, I'm still learning new things. You can too.

Challenge: Take stock of how you influence others. Do changes need to be made? Let God do it for you.

If God is first in your life, everything else will fall into place.

In 2004, I decided to move to Florida for a life change. I needed to get away from Ohio, the stress, the routines, and even my family in order to really focus on God. I took a teaching position at a middle school in Central Florida. I knew I could do the job; I was just a little lost because I didn't know anyone. It was a culture shock.

When I transferred all of my paperwork and certifications, I really thought that my years of experience in Ohio would transfer to Florida. I didn't realize that Ohio had better benefits and a better pay scale than Florida. I soon found out that they didn't want to accept all of my teaching credentials and wanted to pay me ten thousand dollars less than Ohio. I had already moved. No turning back.

My principal made a few phone calls and retrieved some of the loss, but I still took a hit. It was back to eating soup, ramen noodles, and cereal for a while. I was working extra hours tutoring in the evenings to make up the difference. I was struggling. I wondered why I was here and how was I going to make it? I didn't realize that God had a plan already worked out.

The second year I was here, we received a 6 percent raise. That was awesome! It didn't get me back up to where I needed to be, but it was a start. The next year, we received a 7 percent raise. I was ecstatic! Every little bit helped. The next year, we received an 8 percent raise! Unbelievable! So pretty much, the entire county benefited from me moving to Osceola County. I thanked God every day.

I didn't realize when I was planning to move and what God was going to do. Every day, I woke up expecting something new to happen. God surely had my attention. I was able to eat real food and work fewer hours. My life was evolving. I was still young, so I could keep up with the young teachers.

For the first time in my life, I was playing on a real softball team in a league. I so wanted to do it when I was young and never had the opportunity. I was pretty good at it too. I met so many people and was invited to go out and just hang and chill. I was liked for me, not because of anything else. God blessed me with friends and a family that I learned to love and trust.

I found a good church, doctor, dentist, mechanic…all the necessities for survival. I was enjoying teaching. I had never taught middle school but was really having fun with this age group. I was making a difference in people's lives. I was a positive influence and was helping others. My career took a change too. I went back to school to complete a certification and was moving toward the administrative part of my career. Life was good.

All this being said, it took me actually putting God first in my life in order for Him to show me what He could do for me. Every single need that I had, God took care of it for me. It was just unbelievable the way He opened doors. I walked through. I wasn't afraid. I knew He had my back. My stress lessened. My devotion to God increased. He truly was the center of my life. No one understood that but me.

I allowed Him to take me away from the distractions in my life. It's hard to make that move and sell out to God, but I did. It was one of the biggest leaps of faith I ever attempted on my own. God was the center of my being. He was finally first in my life. All those years I thought He was, He wasn't. Now God was it.

Challenge: Put God at the very center of your life. Trust Him. Surrender to Him. Take a step of faith.

God allows you to go through things so that when you tell someone, "I understand what you're going through," you really do.

One day while in the middle of a math lesson, a young lady raised her hand and then motioned me over to where she was. She handed me a note. I read it. In her own words, she told me that she had been raped by her grandfather when she was a little girl. I teach eighth grade, so that couldn't have been too many years earlier. My heart sank. I leaned over to her and said, "When the bell rings, hang back so we can talk."

All the kids left the room, and there we were. I didn't feel uncomfortable talking with her; I just didn't know how to start the conversation. I thanked her for being brave enough to tell someone. She said she was getting counseling and doing better with it. I listened. I wanted to cry. I told her that I truly understood what she was talking about. I told her I was abused by a friend of the family when I was young.

She was calm and not hesitant to tell me that she no longer had contact with the man and was safe now. She seemed at ease talking about it. I listened. I reassured her that I would keep her situation in confidence and that if she ever needed to talk, I was there for her. I told her my room was a safe place to come and chill if she was having a bad day. She didn't even have to say anything; she could just come in, sit down, and relax. She thanked me. I hugged her tightly before sending her out the door. I was glad I was able to be there for her.

Over the years, I've had colleagues talk with me in confidence about being sexually abused as a child. Then they would say, "I don't know why I'm even telling you this." I knew because God had placed them in my path in order to be there for them. I would tell them I truly understood what they were going through and then shared my story with them. These were impromptu conversations while reviewing math for a teacher exam they had to take. It was in different schools where I taught. God placed me where I needed to be for someone to find me and make a connection.

Several years ago, I had the opportunity to be with a friend who was dying of breast cancer. We met while taking classes for certification. I'll never forget getting the call that she was in the hospital and very ill. Immediately, I was there for her. I visited her almost daily while she was getting diagnoses and treatments. After she went home, I would go visit often and sometimes even stay with her on the weekends so her husband could take a break. My heart broke for her. She had given so much of herself and loved everyone she knew. I felt helpless.

As her health deteriorated, I was there for her. I would be brave around her and then cry all the way home. Over the years, the cancer had spread to other parts of her body and her brain. She had taken chemo and all the other treatments, but the doctors had done all they could do. I lost my friend.

No one knows what you go through. They don't understand the difficulties of making ends meet or making it through an illness. No one understands what it's like to lose all hope and go through depressions and anxiety because of the worries that trials take you through. No one understands losing loved ones and soul mates and then having to try to function without them. God truly knows.

Because you rise from the ashes, you have a story to tell. You have compassion like no other. Your life story has been a testament to the grace and mercy of God. It's not wasted time. Help others make it.

Challenge: Don't let your pride keep you from sharing your story with others. Be transparent.

Be holy because you are God's image, not because someone chose to change you.

Believe it or not, there are several thoughts on what being holy really means. Some think that the outward appearance of a person demonstrates holiness. The plainer and more set apart from the world that an individual is, the more holy. Some believe that those who regularly attend church and give abundantly are holy and at the front of the line for the pearly gates. Church organizations accept large donations from wealthy people and feed their egos into believing that they are close to sainthood. In fact, it's none of these.

The Bible tells us to be holy because we are of God and God is holy. There are no specifications listed. There's nothing that tells us that we have to dress a certain way or hang out with certain people to be holy. God is holy. We were made in the image of God. Can we really look like Him? I don't think so. We can't physically look like Him in appearance, but we are called to be like Him in spirit. Think about the characteristics that He possesses. Then model them.

Jesus gave us the beatitudes to live by in Matthew 5. Blessed are the poor in spirit, those who mourn, the meek, those who hunger and thirst for righteousness, the merciful, the pure in heart, the peacemakers, those who are persecuted for righteousness' sake, and those who stand up for God and are treated badly for it. Do these things give you a good picture of God? Jesus was God's Son. He exhibited the same characteristics of God. If we are to be holy like God, then we are to emulate Jesus. He took on God's characteristics when He came into this world. Jesus was the best example of being holy given to us.

When we read and study the Bible, we learn about who God was by His interactions with people on earth. God was patient most of the time. He had a few do-overs when people didn't listen and wanted to do their own thing. Even the chosen Israelites walked away from Him. All in all, God was patient, long-suffering, gentle, kind, and loving. He could have done more than what was done, but I think He held back at times.

Maybe Jesus had a better understanding of human beings because He took on a bodily form. He was earthly and spiritual at the same time. That's what makes Jesus the greatest example to live by. All we are told about His life is from the earthly ministry that lasted three short years. I think He was trying to jump-start humanity. He was on a mission to save us. God led Him the entire time.

God lived through His Son. God gave His only Son and watched as Jesus was abused and killed. He couldn't watch at one point and turned away. That's a human characteristic. He mourned the death of Jesus and the death of humanity. He was patient and waited. God waited for people to come to Him. They chose not to. Jesus was the conduit for salvation and the ultimate connection to God. It had to be that way; otherwise, we would still be sacrificing animals on the Sabbath to atone for our sins.

People will try to condemn you into holiness. Their perspective has been skewed. Leaders are trying to make sheep into the shepherd instead of leading them. Not all sheep are called to be shepherds. Leaders get wrapped up into the outward appearance and gravity of finances that they lose sight of the holiness of God. Obedience is better than sacrifice. The problem is, who are we being obedient to? If it's not God, then it's not His holiness we're following.

God doesn't need someone to do His job. He can change us all on His own. He places people in leadership positions as shepherds to help us know God better and understand His word. He grows us, not people. He makes us holy because we are His image. He loves us for who we are on the inside.

Challenge: Be holy like God is holy. Ask God to change you. You will grow. Follow Jesus's examples.

Jesus taught us how to pray. His way was different from the past. He opened access to God for everyone.

Back in the Old Testament, the Levitical priests were the ones who prayed to God on the people's behalf. They were chosen from all the tribes of Israel to serve before God as priests in the temple. They were consecrated, dedicated, anointed, and vowed to be set aside for God. They performed the sacrifices for sin and atonement for the people. When the temple was built, the Levites were the ones chosen to perform the duties and be separated from the people for God. The Levites were sustained through the other tribes.

God gave laws to live by for the children of Israel. Moses was the leader who led them out of bondage in Egypt. The holy transformation of the priests took place in the desert when a mobile temple was constructed for God to commune with the people. God had never dwelled in a temple. His presence filled the temple, and the priests were the only ones who could enter the temple. They had very strict rules to follow.

The old laws sustained the Israelites over many centuries. All the Israelites knew was what had been passed down from generation to generation. The issue was that the priests didn't exactly follow the laws as expected. They didn't take their position seriously and in some cases counted themselves as better than the common people. The Pharisees and Sadducees thought themselves more holy than others. They loved praying in public so all could see and hear them. They tried to look the part even though their hearts were not in the right place. Some had defiled the temple and lost focus on God. God had to change things around.

Jesus was born. His job was to save the world. The issue was that the Pharisees and Sadducees didn't like His new ways. They condemned Him for changing things up. The only really big change was that Jesus brought a direct communication for us to God. Jesus was the missing much-needed link for the people. Since the old laws were all anyone knew at the time, Jesus's teachings were very radical. It was actually making the high priests look bad and threatened to take away their elite positions of authority. They were running scared.

Jesus taught us how to pray. "Our Father, Who art in heaven, hallowed be Thy name. Thy kingdom come, Thy will be done on earth as it is in heaven. Give us this day, our daily bread, and forgive us our trespasses as we forgive those to who trespass against us. Lead us not into temptation, for Thine is the kingdom and the power and the glory forever. Amen." This simple prayer went against everything that had been taught up to that point. It was a new teaching. A direct line of communication with God. Jesus was upsetting everything from the old laws. People were in an uproar. It went against everything they knew.

Those who followed Jesus understood His teaching. God had to do something to save the world because of the sin and mess it was in. I can imagine the conversation in heaven to figure out what to do. Jesus respected the old laws and continuously referred back to them. Those who didn't know the laws thought they were new ideas. History was repeating itself. Jesus used the same words of the old prophets, and they didn't even realize it. There was such a gap between the old and new, and God had to fix it.

Jesus opened up a direct line of communication with God. No more did they need to sacrifice. No more did they need a priest to interpret the laws for them. No more did they have to confess their sins to a priest to pray on their behalf. Jesus was the ultimate sacrifice. He was the bridge that connected us to God. Because of Jesus's sacrifice, we can now commune with God anywhere and at any time. We can pray anytime we want to, and God hears us. This is how we establish a personal relationship with God. We may never see Him face-to-face, but we can hear His voice. He still speaks to us. We just have to listen.

Challenge: Establish a personal relationship with God. Pray and talk with Him. He's listening and waiting.

Being a follower of God is pretty black and white. Pick a lane. Lead, follow, or get out of the way.

Many stories in the Bible verify that God would rather us be on one side or the other. The gray area doesn't work too well for Him. He doesn't dwell in the maybe. Either you are for or against Him. The only thing is that God has the power to wipe out entire generations and all of humanity if He wants to start over. When He needs you to do something, He won't ask twice. You have to be ready for the moment. At the same time, however, He is very understanding and patient.

When God gave Moses the Ten Commandments, it was for a reason. He was making the rules for the generations of Israel who had left an idolatrous country and lost their focus on Him. God created and blessed the Israelites as His chosen people. They had it made. All they had to do was obey, and God was setting them up for success. They needed guidance. God gave them ten simple commands to live by. Ten was pretty basic and right to the point. They shouldn't have had too much trouble with them, but they did.

Many times, when God was giving instructions about how to take down an enemy, all they had to do was follow His direction. He specifically told them not to take anything from the cities they devoured but burn it all. What did they do? Took stuff they weren't supposed to. He knew they did and then had to reprimand them. He had to be smacking His head thinking that there was one simple thing you shouldn't have done but you did. Many times, He became so agitated with the Israelites that the goal was to let them go back to Egypt and forget it all. He and Moses had long conversations about what was best at the time.

I'm sure He looks at us the same way. He's given us what we need. He doesn't ask much of us, yet we complain and become angry when He doesn't give us what we want. We are the ones who turn away from Him, not the opposite. I'm sure He wonders why it's so hard for us to be a good Christian on Sunday but not the rest of the week. It's pretty black and white. When we step into that gray area, our focus is gone, and we become intimidated by our surroundings. The next Sunday, we're back at being holier than everyone else.

We live in the world, but we don't have to be of the world. We are called to shine our light for God everywhere we go. We should be the same at our jobs as we are in church. Our patient Christian attitude should flow to someone who cuts us off in traffic when we're running late to work. We have lost our ability to gauge our Christian temperature. We can't be one way and then the other. We can't live in a gray area. We lose our ability to positively influence others and share Christ's message.

Pick a lane. We've all been there when deep tragedy overtakes us to the point where we become angry with God and question His motives. Even through the difficult times, we still need to maintain our self-confidence enough to trust that God still has everything under control. He truly does work everything out for our good. Our ability to praise God when things are going well needs to carry over to our times of deep sorrow when all hope is lost. Following God is not just for a season; it's a lifetime.

When our ability to lead is directed to a position of follower, we still need to maintain our godly integrity to reflect Him. When we have done all we know to do and we become tired and weary, we still need to trust and hope that God has us in the palm of His hand. We choose to walk away from Him and take up residency in the gray area. We give in to the pressure to perform instead of applying the pressure. As followers of Christ, we have a choice. We can be really good at it or really bad at it. Choose the good.

Challenge: Lead others to God. Choose to be so transparent that people see God through you. If you have to follow, do it willingly. Avoid the gray area.

Is your spiritual veil in place to protect you or hide your loss of intimacy with God?

When the children of Israel left Egypt, they traveled around in the desert for forty years. The purpose of that was to let the unbelievers sort of die off instead of going into the Promised Land. The following generations had to be retrained to know and honor God after living in a country with idol worship. Moses was the chosen leader to take them through. Moses did his best with the help of God.

At one point, Moses was called up on the mountain to talk with God. He was there for forty days and nights. When he was finished with his conversation, he returned to the people. The only thing was that they were afraid of him because his face was glowing after he had been in the presence of God. He and God had a very close relationship. As Moses communed with Him, he didn't realize the transformation had taken place. He put a veil over his face so that the people were less afraid of him.

When Moses was in the presence of God, he didn't wear the veil. When he was in the presence of the people, he did. The veil was sort of a protection for him. In order to be the leader, he had to be approachable. The only way that could be done was if he wore the veil. In God's presence, he took on the shining glory that emitted from Him. He just soaked up the rays.

This was how Moses lived for a long time. Even after Moses was getting up in years and maybe losing his zest to serve, he still wore the veil. It masked the fact that he was tired and spent after so many years of service. Maybe he didn't want the people to see how he was aging or let them lose confidence in his ability to lead them. I'm sure his relationship with God was the same, but he was just tired. God loved Moses so much that he put his body to rest in a place where no one even knows today.

Sometimes in our Christian walk, we are so full of the spirit of God that we exude His presence in a big way. People notice our enthusiasm and zest for the ministry and look to us as spiritual examples and leaders. As new Christians, we get so excited about sharing the love of God with everyone that we don't recognize the transformation ourselves. People notice that something different has happened to us and we're changed individuals. It's noticeable because we have a spiritual glow about us.

Have we ever used a spiritual veil to cover our weaknesses? When we lessen our communication with God and our relationship becomes stale, do we pull it down further over us to hide our shame and insecurities? Having that spiritual veil allows us to pretend that we are all good, but in fact maybe we have lost our spiritual footing. We still want others to admire us as leaders and strong believers, but we don't want them to see the true us. We hide it.

Too many spiritual leaders have lost their spiritual influence because of trying to please people instead of focusing on God. Their beliefs haven't changed, but their focus has. Where once they had the glow of God, the veil now covers the broken relationship with Him. Yet they still hold positions of authority in hopes that people will follow and revere them. They seem to be more concerned with what people think than what they know. The once powerful message has been whittled down to bare essentials. They've lost their zeal.

It's too easy to pull the spiritual veil over us to cover our inadequacies. We are of the world for a purpose. We need to let God shine through us. No veil means we are held accountable to God. Our lives need to be full of God and our focus clearly on Him. No veil needed. When we're done, we step down.

Challenge: Don't hide behind a spiritual veil. Strengthen your relationship with God so that His light still shines within you.

Every natural, beautiful, priceless pearl started from a small, worthless, insignificant irritant.

Natural pearls are magnificent pieces of raw beauty. The process for creating a pearl is very simple but also very time-consuming. Oysters are the critical caretakers and pearl producers. The whole process starts with an irritant like a grain of sand or a microscopic parasite. It gets trapped in the layers of the oyster and quickly becomes an irritant. As a way to rid itself of the irritation, an oyster secretes a substance that builds up a protection against the irritant. That substance is referred to as mother-of-pearl or nacre. As time goes on and the irritant is still trapped, it gets totally engulfed with the secretion when more and more layers are added onto it. As more and more mother-of-pearl layers are added, the materials in the secretion form an iridescent gem. The oyster is less irritated because its lining becomes smooth against what started as a microscopic, jagged piece of sand or nasty parasite.

The entire process to produce a pearl can take anywhere from six months up to three to four years. The less time to cultivate the material produces a smaller pearl. The more time the irritant is layered, the larger its size. The larger the size, the more expensive it can become. Depending on the oyster, the colors of pearls will vary. Oysters that age well can produce three or four pearls in its lifetime.

So how does this apply to us? Let's apply this to our Christian walk with God. In this case, Jesus is the oyster, God is the cultivator, and we are a pathetic parasite or grain of sand. The mother-of-pearl is the protective layer that Jesus surrounds us in. We start off as new Christians after we accept Jesus into our lives. We are all looking for validation on our spiritual road to heaven. Sometimes, as a new Christian, we get caught up in things where we can't free ourselves.

We vow to do our best and stay devoted to God and His word, but we still keep looking back at our past as a reference point. Sometimes, the temptation becomes so real that we revert back to our old habits instead of moving forward. We're not quite sure where to go and who to follow, so we land in one spot, waiting motionless.

Our devotion is there, but we're still having trouble fitting into a new role.

Jesus sees our dilemma. He sees the jagged edges and our inability to try to fit in somewhere. We're not stable and sure of ourselves so we may be irritating those around us who are watching us flounder on our new spiritual journey. Others are waiting for us to spiritually grow and refine our walk with God. It can be frustrating to others who advise us which direction to go but see us try it our own way. We repeatedly struggle with our new spiritual legs of faith. Others stand and wait, praying for our stability. God waits.

After many months, or even years, the time is right. God has watched us grow. He has left us in the hands of His Son, Jesus, to protect us as we mature. We emerge as a beautiful iridescent gem. We may still be a little jagged, but now God does His part on us. He smooths out our surfaces and shapes us a little. He shines us up and presents us to the world as His priceless possession. We are pearls of great price.

Our maturity process might take months or even years. Our Christian walk is never-ending and yet always full of reshaping and learning experiences. We need time to grow. It's a continuous process. When we lose our shimmer, God shines us up again by building our faith. We're always in His care. Our irritating, immature phase has gone away as we continue to grow and let Jesus shine through us.

Challenge: Take a look at your spiritual progress. Are you truly an extension of Jesus right now?

God doesn't care what you look like when you make it to Him; just get to Him.

When Jesus was preaching, His goal was to reach as many people as possible. I have often wondered if He even knew how long His mission would be. Once Jesus began preaching and performed the first miracle at Cana, His ministry lasted only three short years. There's so much of Jesus's life that is left to ponder because there is no record of what the early years of His life were like. I can't imagine being Him, knowing God was His father, and still trying to be a teenager. It blows my mind.

When Jesus began preaching, He turned the world upside down. His philosophical views were so different from what was taught and believed during the time. His teachings were somewhat contrary to the Old Testament, which was specifically what the Jews followed up to that point. The world was different. Jesus was different. He drew people in just because of His personality.

In the beginning, no one had even heard of Jesus. The disciples were asked to leave everything and follow Him. They did. I'm sure they wondered why at times, but they did. They were with Him, listening to His words and hearing the stories before they even saw the first miracle. That had to be eye-opening for them. The disciples saw how Jesus drew in all kinds of people. It wasn't just the elite; it was the poor too. It was the sick, destitute, homeless, mentally deranged, and demon possessed.

Actually, more of His time was spent with the poor and destitute. It had to have been so frustrating talking with the philosophers and teachers who didn't accept His words and promises. They were probably intimidated by Him and were losing credibility with the public. Jesus loved everyone. He loved and adored the children as well as the adults. He showed mercy to the rich and the poor. Jesus was the gate to God. He was the promise from the Old Testament, and many didn't even believe it. Think about all that they missed out on just because of their unbelief. The poor, sick, and helpless had nothing to lose. They went for it all.

Jesus was the representation of God on earth. God was dealing with a whole new generation that had long forgotten the old ways. This generation was caught up in religion and customs that helped them get nowhere. It was comfortable for them, I'm sure. They probably thought they didn't need some new philosophy upsetting the "good" ways they had established. Life was good for them, so they thought.

Jesus didn't turn anyone away. He took them as they were. People followed Him, just because there was something about this man that drew them in. I'm sure those who were the avid followers had been ignored by society and mostly everyone around them. They had little hope their lives would be better. They honestly put their hope and trust in Jesus. They left everything to follow Him. What a powerful statement.

Fast-forward about two thousand years. Here we are. We are the extension of God. Do we dictate who can and can't get to God? Do we stand in the way of someone's progress toward knowing God? Do we discourage others from finding God because of religion? Yes, it happens. We could easily be a conduit to God if we wanted to. If we can't get close to God, how do we lead others to Him?

God doesn't care what you look like, where you came from, how rich or poor you are, your social status, or how many friends you have on social media. He says to come as you are. There are no stipulations. There are no customs or rituals. There is a direct line to God. We have to get over the stigmas and self-conscious emotions that hold us back. No one dictates your relationship with God. He just wants that relationship with you. If you wait to make the move, you're missing out on life. Get going.

Challenge: Don't hinder someone's progress to God. Don't limit your relationship with Him either.

Desiring to have what someone else does leaves you unappreciative of what you've been given.

Watching others be blessed always makes me feel good. Sometimes, I wonder why others are blessed so much and I have what I do. I totally understand that those who win the lottery faithfully play the lottery. I, on the other hand, play sometimes when extra places are added and it's into the millions. I think, *Why couldn't I be the lucky one to win?* Then I never do. I know God has a reason; I'm just not sure why yet.

Do I really need any more than what I have? Probably not. I am blessed in ways that supersede your average material items. I know that. Would it be nice to not have to work or just retire early in a beach house on an island that I own? Yes, but not yet. So I continue to be blessed by seeing the needs of others being met. I enjoy watching them so thankful and grateful for what seem like miracles to them.

I have never really desired anything that any of my friends or family have. I'm talking about material benefits. I have come to the conclusion that if God knows that I need it, then I will have it. Until then, I live life as is and very simplified. One of the last of the commandments warns against coveting something that another person has. I always thought it meant to just want something. The word itself, though, is described as wrongfully desiring another's property without regard for their rights. So I think back again to the children of Israel and why this was made into a commandment.

Thousands of people walked out of Egypt with the clothes on their back and what they could carry. They may have had nice houses, carts, gardens, and even servants. When they left it all behind, they were limited to very few necessary items. I can imagine that they desired to have the things they left behind. That may have been one reason they kept complaining and wanting to return to Egypt. Their eyes were set on what material things they had.

So after wandering around in the desert for so long, they still didn't accumulate stuff. The same shoes they walked out of Egypt with were the ones that they were still wearing after many years.

Their clothes were the same. Chances are, maybe, that when they left with their few belongings, they really didn't take the good stuff. So in the desert, their neighbors and friends had better goods than them. They desired to have the things their neighbors had. They may have desired their things so much that they were willing to take them or even kill for them. I'm sure they were getting stir-crazy in the heat.

God specifically said to not covet their neighbors' animals, servants, or even belongings. Evidently, something must have been happening. So let's bring it to the present day. There are people in this world who think that they have to have the best of everything. With them, it may be a status symbol. It's a delusion that they actually have money but really don't. If they think they are being outdone by others, they increase their goods. They buy a newer car, or they move into a newer and larger home.

There's a difference between keeping up social status and actually coveting someone's property. Are you willing to gain it unlawfully? Are you willing to wrongfully take someone's property without permission because you just have to have it? Will you try to take what you want by any means possible without the regard for ownership? If you answered yes, then you are coveting.

On the flip side, let's look at how blessed we are instead of what we think we need to have. God has given so much in our lives. The joy, peace, mercy, grace, and love come from Him. Think about those things. Be thankful and gracious for what God has blessed you with. It's all His, anyway.

Challenge: Step back, and take inventory of your blessings before you desire something you don't need.

We all started as a lump of clay. God shaped us and formed us into what He needs us to be. He fixes the cracks too.

Watching someone work with clay is so interesting. The wheel turns, and the lump rotates around the axis. As the potter touches the lump, it begins to take form. The potter knows exactly where to place his hands so that a specific dip in the clay or ridge can be formed. When you're watching the process, it's really hard to figure out what the end product will be. So you watch some more just waiting for the finale.

We are the clay. I picture God patiently sitting at a wheel with a lump of clay in His hands. He knows the end product. He knows what has to be done to make it perfect the way He wants it. He can speed up the wheel or slow it down. He adds more clay or maybe some water to moisten it. Details are added that cause the lump to take form and become something only His eyes can see.

Sometimes, there's a flaw, so He squeezes the clay into a lump and starts again. The process starts all over. Sometimes, He leaves the flaws and continues with the process. Those are the delicate vessels that need special attention. They will still go through the fire and come out more beautiful than the rest. He knows.

Through the process, the clay becomes a vessel. It's delicate to the touch until it goes through the fire. It's at that point that it can be colored or painted on the surface or go directly into the fire. The firing process hardens the vessel so that it can withstand wear and tear. The temperature of the fire is extremely hot and requires the right amount of time in order for the vessel to be hardened for use. The fire brings out the vibrant colors of paint on the surface.

The end product is a beautiful masterpiece of design. No other piece will be exactly the same. Hand-painted designs express the potter's ideas and thoughts. No two can be painted exactly the same. Each piece is unique. Each vessel has its own special purpose and use.

God has a specific design for each of us. There is no one in this world exactly like you. You are unique. You have been designed as a vessel with a purpose. You have been prepared with a specific use in mind. You started as a lump of clay in the potter's hands and shaped into a beautiful vessel for His use. God knows that you are wonderfully and beautifully made.

Think about the different vessels that God creates. All have to go through the firing process to make them usable. The fire hardens the clay to be able to withstand the environment. Think about the extremely hot fire that the vessel has to endure in order to be a beautiful piece of art. Unique in its own way. Brilliant and recognizable for use.

Yes, we have to endure the fires that we encounter. Through the fire, though, we are tested, tried, and hardened, and come out shining more amazingly beautiful than when we started. God allows us to be tested to help us endure our situations and completely trust Him. A worthy vessel is ready to use and willing to go where it's needed. We are the chosen vessels of God. Sometimes, we have to go through the firing process twice. The good thing is that our flaws and imperfections become less noticeable.

When we get cracked because of usage, God is the potter Who mends us. He fixes the flaws and seals us. He knows everything about us. He knows our weaknesses. He patches us up, repaints our exterior, and makes us available for usage again.

Challenge: When you go through the fire, remember that the outcome will be more beautiful than you expected. You can endure the high heat. Let it harden you to be strong.

When you get tired of fighting your battle alone, there will be someone around to hold you up. Let them. Teamwork is easier.

How many times have you fought through a predicament alone and truly wished there was someone around who understood what you were going through? You're not alone. Being alone and fighting through emotional or physical pain can be exhausting. Sometimes, you get to the point where you would rather just give up than go on. Trust me, I've been there more than once. Just because you're a Christian doesn't mean you have a "get out of trouble free" card.

What you have to remember is that there is always someone around who truly understands your pain and situation. There will always be someone there who will lift you up and encourage you. When you get tired of fighting, they fight for you. Maybe not physically but spiritually. That's your ally.

When Moses led the Israelites into the wilderness that God promised, they did nothing more than complain. They had finally reached the point where God was going to give them the land He promised, but they did have to fight for it. They failed to see what God had done for them, and previous generations had lost sight of God in Egypt. These people wanted to go home and be slaves instead of fight. Moses led them into battle.

He positioned himself on a hill overseeing the battle between the Israelites and the enemy. Moses stretched out his rod in the direction of the Israelites and prayed for them through the battle. His arms got tired. When that happened, the Israelites began losing the fight. He lifted his arms again, and they were winning. This was going on for hours. Of course he was tired of holding his arms up, but he had to.

When others around him saw what was going on, they pulled over a rock for him to sit on and rest. He had been standing all day. They each took one of Moses's arms and held it up toward the battlefield. As long as his arms were up and extended, the Israelites were winning. This had to be a team effort. I can imagine even the guys holding the arms had to switch off, too, after a certain amount of time.

The Israelites won the battle and began their journey of overtaking enemy after enemy. Their reputation spread throughout the area, and great armies feared them. Some countries didn't even want the Israelites to pass through their land, because they knew what power they had. Teamwork.

When you go through a battle where your spiritual arms get tired, let others hold them up. God places great prayer warriors in our path to bless us and fight for us. That victory usually comes on our knees with prayer and intercession for others. Don't be ashamed to let someone know that you need prayer or spiritual help. Reach out to those around you. Fighting a battle is always easier with someone by your side. It takes a team to fight against some situations. When you just can't fight alone, someone will be there.

Always be open to the needs of others too. When you come out victorious, you have renewed faith and strength to win again. Your momentum carries over to others. Your victory is a testimony of what God can do. Your joy affects others. Be that teammate for some individual who is struggling alone. You don't have to look very far. God can place someone in need in your path. Be ready and look for the opportunity.

Challenge: Let others help you through your time of need. Don't be so proud that you think you have to make it on your own. God places others around us to spiritually hold us up.

Any foe can be approached and defeated with a heart that's truly set on God.

One of the most prolific stories in the Bible is of David and Goliath. David was just a teenager when he approached Goliath on the battlefield. David wasn't actually in the battle; he was visiting his brothers and taking a report back to their father about the war. Goliath was a giant. He was the enemy's greatest asset. The enemy had the Israelites trapped into thinking that there was no way they could defeat them with Goliath in the lead.

When Goliath defied God and mocked the children of Israel, David was pretty upset. He couldn't believe that grown men were standing around letting this giant speak ill of his God. David had a heart for God. David was a shepherd. He was a true leader. He hadn't even reached his full potential when God called Him into service. David didn't know anything less than God's goodness. He approached Goliath with a sling and three small stones. All it took was one to defeat Goliath. He had mocked God for the last time. He was dead.

God's army moved forward and drove out the Philistines. I can imagine that Goliath's body was used as a stepping-stone to get to the rest of the army as the Israelites took over. They were done. Defeated.

Imagine approaching an uncomfortable situation with a heart set on God. No fear. No worries. No regrets. Just knowing that God has already set a plan in motion and the situation had already been taken care of before you even got there would be refreshing. You would be more likely to approach any situation with amazing confidence and self-esteem. That's exactly how David felt. Why he picked up three stones instead of one baffles me. He probably knew one would do it.

A foe doesn't have to be a physical person. It can be an addiction or a situation, or even nature. We can battle enemies in our physical bodies, our minds, and our emotional senses continuously. How nice would it be to overcome an addiction with confidence that God already defeated it for you? How nice would it be to have true peace of mind where stress doesn't exist? How nice would it be to know that a physical diagnosis was not fearful, because you knew God had everything under control? How do we get to the point that we don't worry?

We can follow David's example. David was on his own in the fields for days at a time. I can only imagine his total focus being on God. I can hear the conversations that he had with God about life. I can imagine how David played music for God and wrote songs of praise and worship that were meant only for God. David knew God in a way that not many people can manage to get to. David wasn't perfect by any means, but his total trust and confidence were in God. David knew that no matter the situation, God had his back.

When we get to the point that we can completely trust in God without fear, hesitation, or reservation, we're pretty close. Those who are closest to God with complete trust are children. They don't know anything but trust. They don't understand anything except the goodness of God. David was a teenager. He must have grown up with complete admiration for God. God was his best friend. When He messed up, he knew that God still loved him with unconditional love, just like that of a child.

Find that place with God where you have complete trust and confidence in Him. The enemy will try to trash-talk you, but you have one more stone in your bag just waiting for the right time. Goliath wasn't killed with a stone; he was killed with faith.

Challenge: Arm yourself with God. Truly trust in Him that no matter what you face, you have the victory. Don't listen to an enemy that talks defeat. You already won!

When your manna stops coming, that means God has brought you to a place where you can survive on your own resources.

When God led the children of Israel out of Egypt, He had a plan. They didn't really understand and would have probably preferred staying in bondage rather than wandering around in the desert for forty years. God had to perform a cleansing. He had taken care of the Israelites since conception. The desert move was to see who truly loved Him, trusted Him, and believed Him after they had been influenced by other religions in Egypt. So when their food ran out after a few days, of course, they complained.

God sent manna into their camps for food. It was actually like sweet honey water. Every morning, the manna would cover the ground. All they had to do was pick it up. The problem was that they complained again because that was all they were eating. There was no meat. Then God sent quails to them. They complained again because that was the only kind of meat that was available in their situation. I can see God just smacking His head over frustration and thinking He should have left them in Egypt.

After God led them into the Promised Land flowing with milk and honey, He had cleared out most of the unbelievers and started fresh with a new generation that trusted Him. It took forty years and many changes to get them where He needed them to be. If He had allowed them to go into the land set aside for them while they were bickering and complaining, they wouldn't have been unified enough to trust that He would give them victories. His timing was very precise. He had a plan.

Once they saw the blessings in the new land that God prepared for them, the manna and quails stopped coming. They had built up enough trust and resources from the new land to sustain their families. For forty years, God had to fix their thinking. They had been so far away from Him when they first started out from Egypt that many wanted to turn back. Even when they saw the grapes from the Promised Land that were the size of coconuts, they doubted that they could take the land. Head smack number two.

It took the old generation dying off and the younger generation to see God's vision in victory. God said He would multiply the people as the sands of the seas. Can you imagine that throng of people coming out of the desert ready to eat? The young leaders marched forward and took the reins for God's plan to be in place. The Israelites conquered anyone in their way. They had enough land and resources to provide for their families many times over. They rested, and they knew God.

God allows you to grow to a certain point, and then it's time to move on. The "moving on" part can be challenging. Some people don't make it. They complain that God gave up on them or doesn't hear them anymore. God simply removed their manna and quails. He would never allow you to go into a situation without having a set, clear plan. How you get there is up to you. You may wander in the desert for a while, but eventually, your manna is going to run out. God has you where you need to be.

You can choose to trust Him or leave Him. You can choose to let the oppressing convictions die and pick up peace of mind. You get to choose your way through your journey. Whenever God decides to send you out a little further, however, it's because He's expecting you to grow and use the resources He's blessed you with. It's your choice to take what He gives you or die in the desert. He knows what He's doing.

Challenge: Grow in the resources God has blessed you with. He expects you to make it on your own two feet. You rely on Him, but you still have to grow in Him.

All it takes is one shot to bring a giant down in your life. When God is the weapon, you can't lose.

We've all been there under the magnanimous feeling of defeat and uncertainty. You feel like you're going down and there's just no way out. Then from somewhere way down deep inside, you find the faith and courage to go after what ails you. That's your giant. The thing that nags and irritates you. That continuous voice of doubt that defies God and makes you question where He is when you need Him the most haunts you. You're ready to give up; but then you muster your strength, defy the odds, and give it one last try.

The Old Testament story about David gives us hope that God does amazing things to accomplish His purpose and show that He is in control. At a very early age, David was anointed to be king over Israel, God's chosen people. He was just a shepherd boy when it happened. Most people wrote David off as anything important, because all he did all day was tend his sheep. They didn't realize that in the quiet times, he communed with God. David had a special relationship with God. He was chosen by God to fulfill a promise.

While David was out in fields watching over his sheep, God was shaping him into a vessel to be used. David had protected his sheep to the point that he killed a bear and a lion with his bare hands. That's amazing faith and trust in God. David and God were one-on-one much of the time. God was pleased with David and knew his heart. As David grew, he realized the value of being a leader and mostly being a protector.

The Israelites had come into a new land. Many of the nations that surrounded them were jealous and continuously tried to overcome them in battle. The Philistines were an ominous foe. Battle after battle, they came back at the Israelites, only to be pushed back time after time. You don't mess with God's chosen people and live to talk about it. So here they came again. This time, they put their mightiest warrior on the front line. His name was Goliath. He was a huge, beastly man. Goliath was a giant.

When David went to the battlefield to check on his brothers, the most amazing thing happened. The battle was at a standstill because Goliath was threatening everyone and defying God. No one had the guts to shut him up. David entered stage right. He questioned who this person defying God was and why no one was doing anything about it. Then he stepped up to service. He couldn't wear the armor, so he headed toward Goliath with no protection. On the way, he picked up five smooth stones. Can you imagine the conversation he was having with God on the way there? No one understood his relationship with God and the power of His might.

Get the visual—Goliath, about nine feet tall, and David, about six feet tall, squaring off. Goliath cursed and defied God and mocked David. He just listened. Then he pulled out his slingshot, loaded it up, and refuted Goliath. He laughed at David but wasn't expecting the next move. David hurled a stone at Goliath which landed directly between his eyes. The power of God in the stone caused a major impact, and Goliath fell. David grabbed Goliath's sword and cut his head off with it. That caused quite a stir. Now he had the backing of the Israelites. One giant stood in the way of victory. It was an easy fix with God in the mix.

When you are so overwhelmed by the giant in your life, load up and get ready. We allow fear to distract us when we know all along that God has our back. We have to get to the point that our complete faith and trust in God are genuine. As Christians, we possess the power of God. There is no enemy that can defeat us. There is no foe that can overcome us. *We have God!* Lose the doubt and fear. Lose the depression and oppression. Live like God has everything under control, because He does!

Don't be defeated. Stand tall and hit the mark. With God, *all* things are possible. Live it!

Challenge: Identify the giant in your life. Connect with God. Trust that He has your back.

When the damage has been done, God uses it for good. He has a purpose in everything.

Sometimes, you may get to that point in your life when you're wondering what's the use in going on. Situations are just too overwhelming. You've lost your zeal to fight; and giving up, it appears, is your only option. You have two options. You can give up, roll over, and die; or you can look forward to the outcome of a bad situation. It's never really fun to be in a bad predicament, but God uses bad situations for His good. You just have to wait on His timing. It's all part of a plan.

Father Abraham had been promised by God that the Israelite nation would grow to unmeasurable numbers. God told Abraham that the generations of people would be as the stars in the sky. That's a big promise, especially to a man whose wife was ninety years old and had no children. She was pretty shocked to hear the news. Abraham trusted God. At ninety years old, his wife gave birth to Isaac. The promise began.

Abraham's grandson Jacob had twelve sons. They became the twelve tribes of Israel. The eleventh son, Joseph, turned out to be his favorite. The older brothers despised Joseph because they knew how much he was favored. Joseph has also been gifted with the ability to interpret dreams. Some of the things he told others didn't go over so well. They had enough. They wanted to kill him. The oldest brother decided he shouldn't be killed but taught a lesson. They put Joseph into a pit in the middle of nowhere and then sold him as a slave to a passing Egyptian caravan. The brothers bloodied his special coat that Jacob had made for Joseph and sent it back to their father. He was heartbroken. God's promise was still in the works.

Joseph ended up in Egypt and working for the king. He was well trusted and honored. A little mishap with the king's wife landed him in prison. She falsely accused him. After he interpreted the Pharaoh's dream, he was now revered by the king and set as second-in-command. He interpreted another one of the king's dreams and prepared for a famine in the land. Joseph was put in charge of the entire country. His family didn't know he was alive or even that he held such power, but they needed food, so off to Egypt they went.

After a couple of trips between Egypt and the family, Joseph recognized his brothers and longed to tell them who he was. Eventually, his identity was found out, and they had a feast to celebrate. They bowed to Joseph, as he had told them in a dream. What they meant for evil God meant for good. Joseph had been secured in a wealthy nation to be able to fulfill God's promise to bless the Israelites. I'm sure there were times when he thought it couldn't get any worse than it was, but he still trusted God to have his back.

Through a series of events, Joseph was reunited with his family. Eventually, he was able to see his father and move the entire clan to Egypt where he could take care of the family. The Israelites prospered in Egypt under the hand of Joseph. They received the best of everything. Their families were well taken care of from the moment they entered the territory and the Pharaoh wasn't even aware that he also was part of God's plan. They multiplied like the stars in the sky. The promise to Abraham was being fulfilled. How many times do you think they all heard the story of a great nation and never believed it?

When someone does you harm, you have the option of wallowing in the hurt or stepping out. Your life may take you on a different journey, but you have to trust that God's plan is in motion. You can stay in your prison or look for opportunities to flourish and step up. Embrace what God has for you. It may not always be what you want, so be accepting of His will in your life. Sometimes, it takes a spiritual earthquake to move you out of your comfort zone. Don't be afraid. You will get used to your new surroundings. You will prosper.

Challenge: Reevaluate your situation. Is there some good coming out of it? Did you reach someone else?

You can have everything in the world and still be miserable. Losing it all helps you refocus.

King David was a mighty man of God. He led God's chosen people for many years. By then, however, the tribes had split up. He was from the tribe of Judah, and his lineage produced Jesus of Nazareth in the New Testament. David was a man after God's own heart. He was a great warrior and so very loved by the people. David ruled for many years. He wanted to build a temple for God to dwell in. After the Israelites had been wandering in the desert for forty years, they finally settled down. David began the plans for the temple. It was not to be built by him but by his successor and son, Solomon.

Solomon was appointed king after David passed away. God had even greater plans for the Israelites. After taking the throne, Solomon followed in David's footsteps and honored God. His job would be to build the temple. One night, Solomon had a dream where God asked him what he wanted in order to better serve the people. He wasn't selfish. He asked God for wisdom to be able to rule the people fairly. God actually granted his desire and gave Solomon wisdom. God also gave him wealth.

Solomon was known for his wisdom and great wealth. The kings around him actually admired him and sent materials to build the temple. They sent skilled laborers to help with the construction. The temple was a huge undertaking, but Solomon was provided with everything. He was given gold and silver to make the utensils and instruments that would be used by the priests. God had prepared the hearts of others to build a place for him to dwell. All who met Solomon were enamored by his wisdom and ability to rule fairly. He wasn't selfish at all. Solomon also had a heart for God and loved Him.

Solomon loved women. He had eight hundred wives. Yes, I said that correctly. The kingdoms around Jerusalem were not all about God. Some had worshiped idols and gods for centuries. It was all they knew. They didn't really know God. When Solomon took women from other countries to be his wives, they brought their pagan worship to the holy city of God. They pleaded with Solomon to let them worship idols and the gods they were used to. He obliged them and set up gardens and areas for many different pagan gods. That was his downfall. Can you imagine trying to make eight hundred wives happy?

Solomon started off his reign with legitimate love for God. I'm sure he continued to love God but was also influenced by his wives. I don't think that his wealth made him any different. He seemed to be a kind and loving ruler even having more than he needed. His kingdom was infiltrated by pagan worship. Because he truly loved women, they turned his focus away from God. It was probably a slow process. Once you give in to one, there are always others behind them trying the same thing.

Solomon built one of the greatest, most magnificent temples in history. It was adorned with the best of everything. It was a showpiece for kings and commoners alike. It was the focal point of Jerusalem. He had accomplished the plan set forth by King David. The temple signified a place for God to permanently dwell among the people. Their journey was over.

Eventually, Solomon's temple was overtaken and destroyed. Everything he had built for God was gone. Solomon had everything he wanted except the ability to control the influence of his wives. He had to be miserable in trying to make sure everyone was happy. His downfall cost him everything.

You can have all the wealth and prestige you need, but if you don't focus on God, it's worth nothing. In the end, your wealth can be your downfall. Some people who have little are still very rich in God.

Challenge: Whatever controls your life influences your outcome. Stay focused on God. He will lead you.

When God tells you to build an ark, don't settle for a rowboat.

God always has a plan in place. Throughout history and the Bible, God had purposes for His people. In the Old Testament, God was more about preserving the Israelites. The Gentiles weren't really even thought about until the New Testament. The stories we read are of those that saved the lineage of Jesus so that we could enjoy the benefits in the New Testament after Jesus came to earth. God loved all of those He created but was especially partial to His chosen ones.

Back in the day, the world had become chaotic. God had created individuals to commune with Him, but not too many had succeeded in pleasing God. Sin was rampant. People had succumbed to pagan worship. They were not adhering to the expectations God set forth. He had to do something to save the lineage of Jesus so that we would also be saved. It's almost like He needed a do-over. People were disrespectful and didn't want to listen.

God chose Noah to do the job. Keep in mind that God may have looked at others to complete the job, but did they have the fortitude and love for God to do it right? Out of all the people on earth, God chose Noah. He knew Noah would listen. He knew Noah's heart. Maybe Noah had a special relationship with God so much that God admired him above the rest. Instructions were given to Noah, and he began building.

Noah wasn't building a canoe or a rowboat. He was building a very large sailing vessel. Noah was scoffed by onlookers. It had to have been the most exciting thing that had happened in a while, so I can imagine people eating lunch and watching the progress. Noah had to listen to their snide remarks. He had to work under intense pressure to complete the specifications given by God. It had to be so overwhelming. Even his family had to endure the ridicule from day to day. God had his back. He pressed on, knowing that God had a plan in place.

The building took months. I'm sure when Noah was asked about the plan on the six o'clock news, he may have been a little bewildered himself. Still, he did the will of God. Noah didn't know what was about to hit them. The ark was finished, God sent the animals as promised, provisions had been made for a long journey, and Noah and his family were safely inside. God shut the door. Noah's gentle spirit did the job. God led him the whole way.

It began to rain. The ark was still idle. It rained more. The ark began to lift a little. The rain kept coming, and the huge vessel began to slowly rise. Looking out the window, Noah knew the amount of water it would take to completely float the boat. He may have even doubted himself at times. Noah heard the cries of the people to save them as the water kept rising. Looking out, there was less land than water. People were perishing in front of his eyes, yet he trusted God.

Forty days and nights passed. Eventually, the waters diminished. Noah, his family, and the animals were saved. Everything else was gone. Think back to the beginning. If Noah had cut corners, the ark wouldn't have been enough to save everyone. He listened to God and trusted Him the entire time. That's how we have to be. God prepares us for situations that we haven't gone through yet.

When God prepares you for something ahead, listen to what He says. Don't settle for less. He knows what's best for you. Don't give up. Don't be swayed by others. It's a trial; you'll be okay. He always knows the outcome. Believe and have faith. God's just growing your faith. He's fulfilling a purpose.

Challenge: When God is preparing you, listen. Listen intently. He's getting you ready. Pray.

The best advice to give to someone in need is sometimes no advice. Ask God to lead you.

Have you ever had someone give you advice except that in some silly way, they were actually making you feel like you deserved what you got? There are those people who actually enjoy saying, "I told you so." In fact, they didn't really know the outcome, nor could they give you solid advice from their lips. They were the kind of friend who should have just kept their mouth shut and let you be. Or what about those people who offer free advice when you didn't ask for it? Again, no, thanks and leave me alone.

In the Old Testament, we learn about a man named Job. He was a very wealthy man for the time. Job owned land and animals and had large prosperous stock investments and a loving family. He was continuously concerned about the well-being of his sons and daughters, so he continuously offered sacrifices on their behalf so that their misdeeds would be forgiven. He was a very loving father.

In one day, Job lost his sons and daughters and his herds of animals, and much of his property was demolished. He had his wife. Job was very well known in his community. He was an upstanding citizen and had a solid reputation. Everyone in the tristate area knew of Job and his wealth. Job's most important possession was God. God knew Job. God knew that Job was a faithful and loving servant. The community was watching to see how Job would respond to the tragedies.

You see, Satan had asked permission of God to test Job. God allowed it because he knew that Job would still be faithful after being tested. Satan had permission to destroy anything in Job's possession, but he couldn't touch Job. That's why the tragedies happened in one. Job did as God expected. He stood strong and never blamed God. He understood that material things could be replaced. He had been freely given everything by God, so if God wanted to take them back, Job understood.

Satan didn't budge Job. He stood tall on his beliefs and revered God. Satan went before God again and asked permission to hurt his body. God responded that it wouldn't matter, because Job was a faithful servant. So Satan attacked Job's body with boils. Job was in pain. He sat in an ash pile and scraped the boils on his skin. All the while, he never complained. Even his wife told Job to curse God and die. He had to put her in her place. Job had nothing against God.

While Job was nursing his wounds, his three friends went to him to console him. Each in their own way gave him advice and an opinion. None of it pleased Job, and he had to reprimand them as well. All the while he was hurting, he was defending God. One of his good friends made it sound like Job had a hidden sin that he was being punished for. Job had been sacrificing daily for sins; how one got missed didn't make sense.

When the three good friends were finished telling Job what they thought, it was God's turn. God spoke to Job and reprimanded the three friends in front of Job. He didn't go easy on Job either. He reminded Job of all that God owned and how he had blessed him. God told Job to get up and be about his business. It was a test of his faith and loyalty to God. Job passed. In return, God blessed him with more children and animals, and even healed his land. Job had even more possessions than he had before.

Sometimes, God allows us to go through things in order to test our faith. We don't always understand what He's doing. If you're a friend to someone in need, be careful of your words of advice. Speak to God before you offer any words of wisdom. God will hold you accountable. If it's not of God, don't say it.

Challenge: Look for the good in your trial. Know that God will bless the situation. Love others through theirs.

Walking on water is the easy part. Meeting Jesus in the middle of a sea is the hard part.

Peter was a simple fisherman. He was one of the first disciples whom Jesus called into ministry. Of the twelve chosen disciples, I believe that Peter was the closest to Jesus. He was certainly a protector and wanted to make sure that Jesus was safe and taken care of. It took him a while to trust that Jesus was the Messiah, but once he believed, he traveled with Him everywhere. Peter became a great asset to Jesus's ministry.

After traveling with Jesus for a while, the disciples really got to see Jesus for Who He was. They learned to trust His voice and follow His commands. The disciples were even part of the miracles that Jesus performed. Their simple actions of faith increased their trust and love for the Messiah. Peter completely trusted Jesus. One evening, he had the opportunity to show it.

Jesus had been preaching to multitudes of people wherever they went. Jesus was teaching but also healing people and trying His best to meet the needs of His followers. Hordes of people flocked around Him all the time. Jesus was constantly surrounded. There were times, however, that He needed to get away and just be alone. Like us, He needed to reenergize Himself and be alone with God.

On one such evening, Jesus instructed the disciples to take the boat and meet Him on the other side of the sea. They obliged and headed out. We're not told much of what the water or wind conditions were. If you've been on a body of water, however, it's isolated from the mainland. Many of the disciples were avid fishermen, so it was unlikely they were in any position to fear the night. We're not told how long it took to get to the other side of the sea, but I'm sure they had work ahead of them.

Can you imagine the disciples in the boat talking about the day's events? They may have been discussing the miracles that took place or certain parables that Jesus spoke to them? They might have even tried to interpret what He meant or how the people related to Jesus. As they toiled along, resting, they heard a voice and saw someone out in the middle of the sea. It's not unusual for someone else to be on the sea, but the voice sounded like Jesus's. They were His transportation, so they might have been a bit confused.

Jesus probably startled them at first. I can see them trying to squint to get a good view of who it was coming toward them. They listened. It was Jesus. He called them. Peter was the only one who asked Jesus if he could join Him. Jesus told Peter to walk toward Him. Without hesitation, Peter climbed out of the boat. The only thing around him was water. Can you imagine the expressions on the other disciples' faces? Peter, the bold and crazy one, was actually getting out of the boat in the middle of the sea. They just watched.

As Jesus drew near, Peter took a step into the water. He didn't sink, though. His other foot landed outside of the boat. He didn't go down. Peter kept His eyes on Jesus and began walking toward Him. Without hesitation, Peter let go of himself and all of the doubts in his mind, and met Jesus on the water in the middle of a sea. Peter had totally surrendered himself to Jesus. His complete trust and confidence were in the Messiah at that point. He was defying the odds. He was walking on water. Jesus steadied him at last.

Think about your situation. Have you ever felt like you were going under and there was no one even remotely close to be able to help you? Then you heard the voice of Jesus. He bade you to come to Him. It's scary to leave your comfort zone. You put all of your faith and trust in Jesus to meet you. You took a step of faith and began your journey. Jesus was there to grab you up and protect you. He's there to calm your fears and steady your walk. Meeting Jesus is the hard part. Being part of a miracle is easy. Have the faith to walk out.

Challenge: Listen. When Jesus calls you out, trust Him. Put everything behind you, and step out in faith.

Don't give into peer pressure unless it's to glorify God. Stand your ground. God has your back.

Solomon had built an elaborate temple in Jerusalem for God. It was the first place the children of Israel could actually call home. They were finally getting settled into the life that God had for them. God had taken them out of Egypt, refocused them under Moses's leadership, and marched them through many enemy camps; and now they were settling in. Because of Solomon's faithfulness, God had allowed peace throughout the land, and Jerusalem had rest. Then things changed a bit.

The change in leadership meant that sometimes the rules changed. When the king's reign ended, someone else stepped in to lead the people. Not every king was approved by God, but that's what the people wanted. Many of the kings had given in to idol worship, which then allowed the children of Israel to be distracted away from God. They wandered far away. God let them be, and the destruction began.

Jerusalem was always the envy of others. Eventually, the city was overtaken, the temple was destroyed, and the Jews were taken into captivity. Many were led out of the city into unknown territories under disloyal kings. Some were taken far away. Their only connection to God was to be able to pray toward the city out of respect and honor. The devoted Jews still had God's heart.

Daniel was one of the young men who were taken captive to Babylon. Daniel loved and honored God. He continued to devote his life to God in spite of his circumstances. The king actually found favor with Daniel and assigned him a powerful position. Daniel still kept God in his heart. Daniel still prayed toward Jerusalem three times a day. He truly loved and trusted God.

The king of Babylon decided that he needed to change things up a bit. He came up with the idea that a statue of himself would be placed in the city for all to see. He also decreed that when the music sounded, everyone would bow down and worship the statue; otherwise, they would be killed. Daniel wasn't about to stoop under peer pressure, so he refused. He continued to open his window three times a day and worship God. It was all good until he was reported to the king. Being a king's servant and not obeying the command didn't go over too well.

Daniel was called in to see the king. He pointed out that he would not bow to anyone but the one and only true God. The king was furious. He had to punish Daniel as an example. He decided to throw him into a den of hungry lions. We all know what hungry lions can do to a man. Daniel may have been a little apprehensive, but his life was worth more by dying for God. He took his punishment. Into the lion's den he went. I'm sure that the king truly loved Daniel and absolutely hated the fact that he had to do the job.

After a while, the king went himself to check on the progress of Daniel's demise. He called out Daniel's name to see if it was over. Daniel happily called back to the king that he was alive and well. The king was taken aback. He didn't expect him to be alive. Daniel proclaimed to the king that the God of Israel had sent an angel to shut the mouths of the lions. He was all good. Daniel was hastily retrieved from the den. The king knew then the power of the living God.

Daniel could have succumbed to peer pressure. It would have been so easy to live, except that Daniel truly loved and honored God. He didn't allow a bad situation to influence his decision to trust God. The next time you are under pressure to conform to something you know isn't right, walk away and stand strong. If God isn't present with you, He will send an angel to guide you. He has your back.

Challenge: Weigh out your decision. Who will benefit the most? Choose good over bad. Choose God.

When God has a job for you to do, He has a very difficult time letting you off the hook.

Jonah was a prophet of God. When I think about those who are chosen to be prophets, I think of their character. I believe that they must be open and willing to go where God needs them to go. They must be willing to be a true extension of God and speak what God needs to be spoken. They must be brave enough to take the ridicule and speculation from those who don't have a close relationship with God.

The people of Nineveh had been spiraling out of control. God had watched what was going on for a while. Jonah wasn't too far away, so He decided to use him on a mission. The people needed to know that God loved them. They had strayed away from all things God and were very misguided by their surroundings. They had walked away from God. They were having a good time but lost the focus on God in the process. He just needed to give them another chance to turn things back around.

God called on Jonah. Jonah was probably very happily sitting at home, catching up with friends, tending his garden, and enjoying life. Jonah knew God, so he had no worries. He respected and honored God. He probably didn't even really care much about what was going on outside of his circle. When God got Jonah's attention, He informed him of his mission. Jonah was, no doubt, traveling way outside of his comfort zone and hesitant about the task. He probably even questioned the details and asked God to repeat them.

The mission from God was that Jonah would go to Nineveh. It was quite a distance away. He had to find transportation and travel a good distance. A boat would be okay. Once he got there, his instructions were to tell the people of Nineveh that God had sent him with a message. The message was that God knew what they were doing. They were to repent of their sins and turn back to God; otherwise, the city would be destroyed. That was pretty simple.

Jonah set off on his mission. He boarded a ship headed toward his destination, except it was not quite exactly where he needed to be going. Jonah was on the run. He avoided the situation. An interesting thing happened, however, and God stirred up a boisterous storm. Everyone in the boat was afraid for their lives, except for Jonah. He was sound asleep in the bowels of the boat. The crew decided Jonah was the problem and threw him overboard. That actually took care of the problem. The storm subsided, and all was well.

Jonah sank into the sea, shocked and trembling, I'm sure. Interestingly enough, God prepared a large fish that swallowed Jonah. He survived. Jonah was trapped in the belly of the whale for three days and nights. Just think about that situation for a minute. I would have loved to have heard the conversation between Jonah and God. I've often wondered why it took three days. Maybe Jonah needed some convincing. I, personally, would have been okay with my mission after the first few minutes.

The large fish hit the beach at Nineveh, was nauseated by Jonah's presence, and threw him up on the sand. Jonah didn't have much time to clean up before making a grand entrance into the city. Imagine seeing this guy covered in seaweed and fishy residue shouting at you to repent and turn back to God or He would destroy the city. I know I would have dropped immediately to my knees and prayed hard. Actually, the people did repent. God spared the city, and Jonah went home. Mission accomplished.

If Jonah had listened to God in the first place, he could have avoided his calamity. You can do the same. Don't make God come chasing after you to get you to listen to Him. You've been blessed by God. The least you can do is take on a task for Him. It's a win-win situation.

Challenge: When God needs you, don't run away. He's trying to reach someone within your grasp.

Jesus is one present that you can regift. He didn't come with a receipt. He's nonreturnable.

Throughout the Old Testament, many prophesied about a Messiah Who would be raised up for the people. For many years, the Jewish people relied on God's words and waited for their Messiah. He was going to be their king and Savior Who would rescue them from persecution. As the years went on, I'm sure their hopes diminished. They believed God's word and the prophecies but expected Him to come in a much different form from what they were even prepared for.

We have all heard the familiar Christmas story told in the gospels of the New Testament. Mary was chosen to give birth to Jesus, who would be the Messiah. She knew it and believed, but not everyone supported her theory. For her to state that God, Himself, would be the Father of a human child seemed unrealistic and preposterous. I'm sure she was shunned and even hidden away because she was just promised to Joseph and was pregnant before they were married. What a scandal that must have created.

When her time to give birth was near, she was in Bethlehem. The Bible tells us that Jesus was born in a manger, around animals and livestock. He came into the world in the meekest and lowly of environments. Mary and Joseph didn't even really have family around to celebrate. They believed Jesus was the Promised One of God. All of heaven rejoiced, God's plan was set into motion, and Jesus had made His way to earth to begin His mission. The long-awaited Messiah had been born.

The shepherds were rejoicing and followed the star of Bethlehem to see the baby king. Not much celebration was happening on earth, because many understood that a king was coming to save them, not a baby. God sent people to honor the birth of Jesus. Wise men and mighty kings came from the east with gold, frankincense, and myrrh. Those gifts were very valuable offerings for such a young ruler. Can you imagine what would have happened if people understood who He really was? As word of mouth spread, people perked up with the possibility that the prophecy was fulfilled. Jesus was born!

The plan that God set into motion had a distinct purpose. Throughout the Old Testament, atonement for sins was acquired through sacrifices. The priests had their hands full performing the duties of sanctifying the offerings and presenting them to God. This was understood by the Israelites as the main connection to God. The new plan would change all of that. God had heard the murmurs of His people for centuries. He had tried to help and lead them, yet they chose to walk away. The Jews prayed for a Messiah to save them.

The only problem was they were given the greatest gift of all, Jesus the Messiah, and they didn't believe He was the true Messiah they had prayed for. Those who believed knew in their hearts that God had come to earth. Those who chose to reject Jesus still waited for a king to come in all of the splendor. How were they going to be led by a baby? Even as a baby, however, Jesus was intimidating to kings. Just the mention of His name sent fear into the hearts of many men. He was there to save them, not hurt them.

God needed a way to reach all people, not just His chosen ones. Jesus would be the ultimate sacrifice for sins. His mission was to reach all people, not just the Jews. God gifted us with a Savior Who would change the world forever. God gave us the greatest gift of all. It's up to us to share the gift with others.

We, as believers, have an obligation to share Jesus. Even if people reject your gift to them, remember that it's not you they reject but God. Freely Jesus was given; freely we receive. He is meant to be regifted. If it wasn't for the birth of Jesus, we wouldn't know God as we do. Let every day be Christmas.

Challenge: Choose someone you know who needs Jesus. Gift them. Freely give Jesus to others.

The greatest sacrifice you can give is yourself. Give freely, and be freely blessed.

Not much is said about the life of Jesus from the time of His amazing birth until the time He began His earthly ministry. At one point, He is found in the temple speaking with the scholars about God. He had been disconnected from the caravan of family returning home. When Mary found Him, Jesus told her that He was being about His Father's business. Mary knew in her heart what He meant. She knew who He really was.

At about age thirty, Jesus revealed Himself by performing miracles and teaching in a way that people were absolutely enthralled by His words. They had never heard the scholars or teachers speak with authority and love the way Jesus did. He drew quite a following quickly. The only problem was that the Romans feared Him. Word spread quickly about a Man Who was healing the sick, loving the people, performing miracles, and even raising the dead. He was accused of blasphemy against God because Jesus said that He was the Son of God. Still, His followers grew rapidly in number.

Many believed He was the Messiah, yet others were still waiting for someone of royalty. The Jews had been told for centuries that God would send them a Savior to lead them. They expected someone to rise up in the earthly ranks of a society that would physically overtake their enemies and lead them in battle. Jesus was pretty much the opposite. He came from a lowly carpenter's household, in a small city. He wasn't well known or hadn't proven Himself among the scholars. Jesus hadn't attended professional schooling to be a prophet or scholar. He just was.

His first miracle was turning water into wine at a marriage feast in Cana. He had already called many of His disciples, so they had seen what He had already been doing for people and glorifying God. At this point, Jesus was it. Word spread quickly from a small wedding ceremony. Since everyone was talking about Jesus, this just cemented the fact that He truly was someone special. Yet the Jews and scholars doubted Him. They were intimidated by His presence and ability to influence anyone He came in contact with. They were mostly afraid of His power.

Jesus spent the next three and half years doing the will of God, His Father. He always knew it would come to an end, so He was fervent in reaching as many people as He possibly could. Jesus not only reached the Jews but every person from every walk of life. His sole mission was to come to earth and provide a way for individuals to know God and have a more intimate relationship with Him. Jesus was the intercessor between humans and God. No more did anyone need to sacrifice for their sins to be atoned and forgiven. They had personal contact with God through Jesus Christ.

Jesus was the way for people to reach God. No one could go to the Father except through Him. This was such a radical idea. He was the Messiah Who had been spoken of in the Old Testament. He was the Savior of the world. He was the ultimate sacrifice for our sins. He was a representative for every person from every walk of life. When people accepted Him, they were spiritually born again. They had a renewed faith and hope. Jesus was so intimidating to the authorities, however, that it cost Him His life. He was crucified.

Let's put all of this in the present tense. Jesus died centuries ago for all of us. When we confess our sins to God and receive forgiveness, we are spiritually saved. If we believe in Jesus and that God raised Him from the dead, our faith is sealed. We become believers in Christ. Our lives take a new journey with God the Father. God now becomes our Heavenly Father. We can approach Him any time through the power of prayer. We don't need another mediator; Jesus already did that for us. We have been grafted into the family of God.

Challenge: Check your life. Are you a godly believer? If not, pray and ask Jesus into your life.

About the Author

Elfie grew up in a small town in Northeast Ohio. She is the youngest of seventeen children. Her passion for reading and writing began at a very early age. Now after a teaching career of thirty-five years, she has many stories to tell.

Elfie has a bachelor's degree in education and a master's degree in education administration and is currently teaching math to eighth graders in Central Florida. She has been recognized for her outstanding teaching career. Elfie has been chosen as the Teacher of the Year for two different schools. She was selected as one of the top ten teachers in Osceola County, Florida, in 2017.

Elfie comes from a very large family. Her passion for teaching extends to the many hundreds of nieces and nephews who call her Aunt Elfie. Her favorite times are spent with family in Ohio in the summer during break. Laughing and telling stories about the family growing up on a small rural farm have brought so much joy. Now those stories extend to you.

Elfie was raised in a Christian home and grew up believing and trusting in God. The stories in this book are told as a result of passion, healing, and respect for God and His word. The stories are written to be an encouragement to every reader and also to challenge you to be the best you can in this world.

You will laugh, you will cry, and you will feel the emotions on this epic journey. Enjoy.

elfie17@comcast.net

CPSIA information can be obtained
at www.ICGtesting.com
Printed in the USA
LVHW051107020322
712194LV00005B/139